WORLD'S DUMBEST CROOKS

AND OTHER TRUE TALES OF BLOOPERS, BOTCHES & BLUNDERS

ALLAN ZULLO

To Dylan Arnold,
a winner in anyone's book

This edition published in 2003.

Originally published under the title *Bloopers, Botches & Blunders*.

Copyright © 1998 by the Wordsellers, Inc.

Published by Troll Communications L.L.C.

Printed in Canada.

10 9 8 7 6 5 4 3 2 1

CONTENTS

GOOFS AND GAFFES

When you've made a big mistake, do you ever wish your life was a videotape so you could rewind it and erase the embarrassing part? We've all suffered those awkward moments. You arrive in class only to discover that you did the wrong assignment. You give a book report in front of the class without realizing a piece of Gummi Bear is stuck between your teeth. When your cute new classmate smiles at you in the cafeteria, you bump into the principal and spill your lunch tray all over her.

So you goofed. Hey, it's okay. You're only human. We all blunder every now and then. But no matter how mortified you get, your goof probably isn't as outrageous as you think. Chances are it would never qualify for Life's Hall of Shame.

Life's Hall of Shame is a mythical place where people are (dis)honored for bungling big time—so big it's worthy of special attention. That's what this book is about. It's a lighthearted look at some of the wackiest, silliest, wildest blunders that have ever happened.

You'll read about everyday people like the man who accidentally blew up his Christmas dinner, the boy whose tongue was stuck on a frozen flagpole, and the woman who mistook glue for eyedrops.

You'll discover that the biggest names in the world of sports have suffered shameful moments—stars like Scottie Pippen, Ken Griffey, Jr., and Wayne Gretzky.

You'll learn that the nuttiest things often happen to not-so-bright criminals—like the burglar who fell asleep on the job, the thieves who were caught videotaping their own crime, or the bank robbers who accidentally locked themselves in the vault.

Above all, you'll learn that it's a blunderful world!

WANTED: DUMB OR ALIVE

AT LEAST THE WITNESS WAS ACCURATE

Thomas Martin, who managed the Jack in the Box restaurant in Oroville, California, in 1996, called police and told them he had been robbed of $307 as he was closing the place.

Martin answered all their questions and then provided police sketch artist Jack Lee with a detailed description of the suspect. Lee was impressed with the witness's memory. Within a matter of minutes, the artist felt confident he had drawn the face of the suspect.

When Lee put his pad down, he suddenly noticed that the drawing looked very much like the victim, Thomas Martin. After further questioning by the police, Martin confessed that he had stolen the money from his own restaurant.

AN ARRESTING PERFORMANCE

A shoplifter swiped $100 worth of film from a Baltimore drugstore, then fled out the door. He sprinted down the street, turned the corner—and ran smack into bad luck. The thief was right in front of two officers whose guns were drawn on a murder suspect lying spread-eagle on the pavement.

"Oh, no!" the shoplifter muttered as he dropped the film and raised his hands, waiting to be arrested.

But the officers weren't real. He had crashed the set of the TV show *Homicide: Life on the Street* during a rehearsal of an arrest scene!

The shoplifter had given himself up to actors Richard Belzer and Clark Johnson, who play Baltimore detectives John Munch and Meldrick Lewis on TV. The actors gave each other a "Now what do we do?" look. They weren't prepared to arrest the man, who continued to stand there with his arms raised.

Luckily, real police officers working overtime as security guards for the production crew soon arrived and took the suspect away.

"If he's convicted," said Johnson of the 1996 incident, "the judge should drop the theft charge and send him away for being stupid."

ALWAYS GET YOUR REST

A burglar fell asleep on the job.

According to New Jersey police, suspect Peter Thomas broke into the Jersey Shore Coin Shop in Ocean City late one night in 1997. Before attempting to steal valuable coins, Thomas sat down on the floor for a little rest.

He quickly fell asleep—and stayed in dreamland until police, who were responding to an alarm, woke him up.

LUCK OF THE DRAW

After buying an Oregon State Lottery ticket, Alice Krumm looked at the winning numbers posted on a sign by the cash register of the store.

To her dismay, she was only one number away from winning $20. Sneaking to the back of the store, she took out a ballpoint pen and changed the number on the lottery ticket. Then she went to the counter to collect her prize.

The clerk spotted the forgery right away and called police, and Krumm was arrested and charged with fraud. Then the arresting officer made a startling discovery. Had Krumm looked more closely at the sign listing the winning numbers, she would have seen that her original ticket had also been a winner—for $5,000!

GEE, WHAT GAVE ME AWAY?

Robber Clive Bunyan put on his darkened full-face motorcycle helmet and entered a store in Cayton, England, where he ordered the clerk to hand over £140 ($225) from the cash register.

Then Bunyan hopped on his motorcycle and sped off. He thought he had pulled off the perfect robbery—except for one small detail. He had forgotten that written across his helmet in inch-high letters was his name, CLIVE BUNYAN. It didn't take police long to catch him.

CHECK THIS OUT

Charles Meriweather broke into a home in Baltimore and ransacked the house. When he could find only $11.50

in cash, he asked his frightened victim, "How do you pay your bills?"

"By check," she replied.

"Okay, write out a check to me for thirty bucks. No, better make that fifty."

"Who should I make it out to?" she asked.

"Charles A. Meriweather," said the robber. "It better not bounce or I'll be back."

He never got the chance to cash it. Meriweather was arrested several hours later.

HE LIGHTED THE WAY

After a clerk at an all-night convenience store near Lawrence, Kansas, reported he had just been robbed by a gunman, police searched the area for the culprit.

Within minutes, two officers spotted a man running in the darkness between houses in a nearby neighborhood. The cops gave chase. The gunman outran them, but he was shocked to see that other officers were now on his tail from a different direction.

He was finally caught. As he was led away, he asked, "How did you catch me?"

One of the officers pointed to the man's high-tech tennis shoes—shoes with heels that blinked on and off every time his feet hit the ground.

A STICKY SITUATION

In 1993, Edilber Guimaraes broke into a glue factory in Belo Horizonte, Brazil.

But before he could steal anything, he was overcome by the fumes and collapsed. As he fell to the floor, he knocked over a tank of glue. When he finally came to, he found himself in a sticky situation—he was glued to the floor!

Unable to tear himself loose, Guimaraes lay there for thirty-six hours before workers discovered him. They called firefighters, who managed to cut him loose. Then the police came and stuck him in jail.

WELL, AT LEAST THEY TOLD THE TRUTH

In 1994, Raymond Cuthbert walked into a drugstore in Vernon, British Columbia, Canada, and boldly announced that he and his partner would rob the place in a half hour. Then he left.

Taking him at his word, the clerk called the Royal Canadian Mounted Police, who waited for the suspects to show up. Sure enough, Cuthbert and his partner, Robert Phimister, returned as promised—and were promptly arrested.

BEHIND BARS

Police in San Antonio, Texas, caught Terry Allen in the act of removing burglar bars from the window of a beauty salon.

Allen was charged with attempted burglary, but he insisted he was guilty only of the lesser charge of theft. He claimed he wasn't trying to break into the beauty salon. He was trying to steal the bars so he could put them on his own windows—to protect himself from burglars!

WELL, BOWL ME OVER!

Amanda Guild bowled so well in a 1990 local tournament in Saginaw, Michigan, that she was named "Bowler of the Week." That meant a story about her, plus a photo, appeared in the *Saginaw News*.

The photo caught the eye of Steven Kurkowski, a U.S. marshal who was glancing through the paper. "We'd been looking for Guild because she was wanted by federal authorities on several serious charges," he recalled.

Months before the tournament, Guild learned the police were after her, so she fled from Tennessee to her hometown of Saginaw. But her whereabouts remained unknown to law enforcement officials until her photo appeared in the newspaper.

"If I was wanted by the police, I certainly wouldn't want my picture in the paper," said Kurkowski.

The week after Guild's best night of bowling, the authorities arrested her at—where else?—the bowling center. Said Kurkowski, "She went from 'Bowler of the Week' to 'Arrest of the Week.'"

VIDE-UH-OH

One was the director, one was the cameraman, and the other four were actors in a live drama captured on videotape.

Only this video camera wasn't taping a scene for a TV movie. It was capturing a real crime—committed by the very people who were involved in the taping!

According to police, six teens from Marana, Arizona, were driving around in a van late one night in 1996. They decided to steal cases of drinks from a service station that doubled as a convenience store. With their video camera running, four of them went into the store, stole the drinks, then hopped back into the van. As it sped off, one of the suspects fired two shots at the attendant but failed to injure him.

The attendant called police, who chased down the suspects and recovered a gun—and the videotape. When police played back the tape, they had all the evidence they needed. The tape showed the suspects in the van planning their theft, then revealed them actually committing the crime.

The thieves made the tape because they had intended to show it to their friends. Instead, these losers learned that their tape would be seen by a jury.

TAKING A BITE OUT OF CRIME

There's a downside to having a unique nickname. Just ask Jimmy Williams, Jr., who goes by the name of Jim Dog.

Williams was arrested in 1996 in New Haven, Connecticut, in connection with a serious brawl. Police suspected Williams when they found a set of gold-plated teeth inscribed "Jim Dog" at the scene of the fight.

NO-BRAINERS

Some criminals are bold in their actions but lame in their lies.

In Columbus, Ohio, in 1996, Charles Kinser and Timothy Lebo stole a car and used it to ram a bank building, jarring loose a 1,000-pound (454-kilogram) automated teller machine. Then they chained the battered

ATM to the rear fender and managed to drag it across the bank parking lot before the police surrounded them.

When the cops asked them what they were doing, the two men said, with straight faces, that they were hauling off an old washing machine! Their absurd story didn't wash with the police, who arrested Kinser and Lebo. Later, the two men pleaded guilty and were each sentenced to up to thirty years in prison.

✷ ✷ ✷

A forty-one-year-old man broke into a home in North Knoxville, Tennessee, in 1996 and demanded a glass of milk. The shaken resident poured the milk as ordered, then secretly called the police.

A few minutes later, the officers arrived, only to hear the suspect deny he had broken into the house and drunk the milk. They didn't believe him—especially since the back door had been broken open . . . and a milk mustache still clung to his upper lip.

FOLLOWING IN HIS FOOTSTEPS

In Columbia, Tennessee, in 1996, Kevin Owens walked into a convenience store early in the morning and demanded money from the clerk. After getting the cash, the bandit stole the clerk's car and drove to the parking lot of an apartment complex.

Unluckily for him, Owens parked next to a large puddle. When he got out, his feet splashed into the water. He then ran and hid in a friend's apartment.

Moments later, the police found the stolen car—and followed the wet footprints right to the apartment, where they arrested Owens.

THE ALMOST-PERFECT PLAN

A father and son in Rome, Italy, thought they had plotted the perfect crime in 1996.

The father worked as a teller at a bank. The son would enter the bank, go to his father's window, and demand money. His father would quickly turn over the cash, the son would flee, and later the two would split the loot. Best of all, no one would get hurt because no weapons would be used.

On the day of the robbery attempt, the young man walked into the bank and went to his father's window. He got the money and ran out of the bank—but he and his father were caught anyway. It seems there was an unfortunate slip of the tongue by the robber. When he was at the teller's window, the crook shouted, "This is a holdup. Hand over the money, Dad."

A STYLISH LAW SUIT

After his arrest on charges of burglarizing a home, Michael Allen of Flint, Michigan, arrived in court in 1994 dressed in a green, double-breasted suit that he hoped would make a good impression on the judge. Allen made an impression, all right!

Pointing to Allen, the victim told the judge, "He's wearing my suit!" An examination of the label of the custom-made suit proved the clothes definitely belonged to the victim.

A FOOL FOR A CLIENT

There's an old saying: A defendant who acts as his own attorney has a fool for a client. The courts are full of such fools.

In a 1985 criminal trial, Michael Blackwell of Bridgeport, Connecticut, acted as his own lawyer. At the end of the two-day trial, he was found guilty of two counts of attempted robbery. The jury took less than an hour to reach its decision.

As soon as the verdict was read, Blackwell told the judge he planned to appeal. When the judge asked him on what grounds, Blackwell replied, "I had a bad lawyer."

* * *

Marshal Cummings, Jr., of Tulsa, Oklahoma, acted as his own attorney at a trial for a purse snatching.

Cummings denied he was the robber. But he couldn't deny he was a lousy lawyer. While questioning the victim, Cummings asked, "Did you get a good look at my face when I took your purse?"

The jury didn't need to hear anything else. Cummings was convicted and sentenced to ten years in prison.

THE WHOLE TRUTH AND NOTHING BUT

During a 1989 case in municipal court in Middletown, Ohio, a lawyer asked the judge to be excused from representing a client.

The judge scanned the courtroom, looking for a suitable replacement. But before he could find one, the defendant stood up and said, "That's all right, Judge. I won't be needing another lawyer. I've decided to tell the truth."

WINNER TAKE ALL

During a 1991 trial, attorney Arlo Sommervold of Sioux Falls, South Dakota, was representing a defendant charged with stealing hogs.

After Sommervold put on a spirited defense, the jury ruled that the defendant was not guilty.

Sommervold turned to shake hands with his client. But the client had an important question. He asked his lawyer, "Does this mean I can keep the hogs?"

GET REAL

Edward McAlea put on a stocking mask, burst into a jewelry store in Liverpool, England, and pointed a revolver at the three men inside. "This is a stickup," he said. "Get down!"

None of them did. They realized he was holding a toy gun when they noticed the red plastic stopper in the muzzle. The men jumped on the would-be robber. After a brief scuffle, McAlea escaped, but not before his mask was pulled off.

The jeweler recognized him as a customer from the day before. Hours later McAlea was arrested.

GOING THE WRONG WEIGH

After tricking the driver of an armored truck into leaving the vehicle one day in 1990, David Posman knocked him on the head with a bottle. Then he ran to the truck and helped himself to four bags of loot.

But when Posman tried to run away with his money, he discovered he had a problem. Each bag weighed 30 pounds (14 kilograms). The 120 pounds (56 kilograms) of weight greatly slowed his escape as he staggered toward his car. Police had little trouble nabbing him in a nearby parking garage. Posman was caught still lugging the money bags—which contained nothing but pennies.

SAFE AT LAST

Three men broke into a bank in West Covina, California, in 1991. That was their first mistake. The bank was empty because it was going to be torn down.

Before leaving, one of the men, John Meacham, walked over to the empty bank vault and suggested his partners step inside to hear the echo of their voices. The two went in while Meacham closed the vault door so they could appreciate the full effect of the sound.

That's when they heard a click. The door had locked. Meacham spent forty minutes trying to open the safe but failed. In desperation, he called the fire department, who informed the police. Seven hours later, after workers broke through the concrete wall, the locked-up robbers were freed—only to be locked up again, this time in jail.

HE JUST COULDN'T RESIST

Daniel Isham, a convicted burglar in Pasadena, California, was on parole at home with an electronic bracelet monitor in 1996. He couldn't stray more than 150 feet (46 meters) from his house or the monitoring device would alert the police.

But Isham thought he could still outsmart the cops. He broke into his next-door neighbor's house. Now he's doing twenty-two years of hard time—in prison.

COUNT HIM OUT

One late afternoon in 1996 in Palm Beach, Florida, Steven Jeffrey Raines walked into Testa's Restaurant, sat down at the bar, and ordered a drink.

He asked bartender Chip Welfeld, "Do you mind if I count out my money at the bar?"

"No, go right ahead," Welfeld replied.

So Raines dumped $10,000 in cash on the bar and began counting.

The bartender got suspicious, especially since he had heard that two banks in Palm Beach had just been robbed. Welfeld called police. They walked into the restaurant just as Raines finished counting his cash. Moments later, Raines was charged with the robbery of the two banks.

A FAILURE TO COMMUNICATE

A masked gunman walked into a snack shop in Amsterdam, capital of The Netherlands, planning to hold up the cashier.

Try as he might, the robber couldn't seem to make it clear to the employee that this was a stickup. No matter how much he threatened or gestured, he couldn't get his point across. Frustrated, the robber was forced to flee empty-handed.

It was just his luck that he entered the shop when the only employee there was a foreigner who spoke little Dutch.

PLEASE DON'T EAT THE DAISIES

Kevin Clifford was really hungry.

With his stomach growling, Clifford, of Stansted, England, walked into a Chinese take-out restaurant one night in 1996 and ordered lots of food.

He paced back and forth, waiting for his order. Meanwhile, the aroma wafting out from the kitchen made him increasingly hungry—and impatient.

Clifford couldn't take it anymore. He had to eat something—anything—right then! His eyes darted around the small waiting area. There was nothing he could munch on except . . . *hmmm*, those potted plants sure looked tempting.

Incredibly, Clifford ripped the leaves off the plants and chowed them down! By the time his order was finally ready, he had eaten the leaves off every plant in the place!

However, Clifford's appetizer turned out to be quite expensive. The restaurant owner took him to court over the loss of the potted plants. The judgment against Clifford was hard to swallow. He had to cough up £437 ($700).

JUST DOING HIS DUTY

One night, Mrs. Hollis Sharpe of Los Angeles was walking her poodle, Jonathan.

After her dog did his business, Mrs. Sharpe used a plastic bag to clean up after him. She was walking home with the bag in her hand when a mugger attacked her from behind. He shoved her to the ground, grabbed her plastic bag, jumped into a car, and drove off. He thought he had stolen something valuable. What a surprise!

Mrs. Sharpe, who suffered a broken arm, said later, "I only wish there had been a little more in the bag."

DOOR-TO-DOOR CONVICT

Billy Williams picked the wrong time and place to escape from jail.

In 1997, the inmate managed to slip out of jail in Valdosta, Georgia. He happened to make his getaway on the coldest night of the year. Not prepared for temperatures that had dipped below freezing, Williams decided to give himself up.

He walked up to a house and asked the resident to call the police. The resident slammed the door in his face. So Williams went next door with the same request—and was met with the same response.

The shivering escapee kept going door-to-door until he finally found someone willing to help him get back behind bars.

WHAT HAVE YOU GOT TO SAY FOR YOURSELF?

A psychic who claimed she could talk to the dead was building up quite a business in Milan, Italy, in 1997.

Madame Mysterioso astounded clients during séances by carrying on conversations with the spirits of departed loved ones. But her psychic chats were soon silenced. During one séance, a client heard someone sneeze under the table where the psychic sat. The client stooped down and discovered a midget, who had been faking the voices of the dead from under the table. The midget and the so-called psychic soon had some talking to do—in court, where they faced charges of fraud.

WHAT'S GOOD FOR THE GOOSE IS GOOD FOR THE GANDER

One day in 1997, Police Officer Steven Rogers of Nutley, New Jersey, saw that a little old lady needed help getting across the street. So he pulled over and helped her.

Then he stepped into a café for a cup of coffee. While he was sipping his drink, he received a call on his police radio. It said a citizen had complained that a car was parked too close to an intersection.

Officer Rogers went to investigate. Sure enough, there was the car, illegally parked. He wrote out a ticket—and then went to City Hall to pay the $17 fine. The illegally parked vehicle was none other than Officer Rogers' patrol car!

THEY GOT WHAT THEY DESERVED

In 1996, police in Acostambo, Peru, chased a carload of thieves until the bandits were surrounded.

The bad guys got out of the car and held up their hands—hands that clutched wads of money. They offered police a deal: "Let us go and you can have all this cash."

Because the police were woefully underpaid, it only took a few seconds to make up their minds. "Sure," they said. After stuffing their pockets with the bribe, the cops waved good-bye to the thieves.

The next morning, police discovered that the cash the bandits had given them was no good. It was all counterfeit!

PAYING TOO STEEP A PRICE

You've heard the expression "crime pays." The truth is, bad guys sometimes pay for their crimes with their lives.

Burglar Salomon Garcia sneaked into a Long Island

real estate and insurance building in the middle of the night in 1996 and tried to break open the safe.

When Garcia failed to crack the safe, he decided to take it with him. That was no easy task, since the safe was on the second floor of the office and weighed about 600 pounds (272 kilograms). But somehow Garcia managed to push the safe out of the room and to the top of the stairs.

Standing a few steps below the safe, Garcia slowly began moving the 2-foot-wide (1.6-meter) by 4-foot-high (1.2-meter) safe down the steps. That's when something went terribly wrong. The safe was too heavy for him to hold. It skidded all the way down the stairs to the bottom.

The next morning, owner Dave Sloop walked into the building and found the burglar—crushed underneath the office safe.

✽ ✽ ✽

When a Los Angeles burglar noticed that a house was being treated for termites, he rubbed his hands in happy anticipation.

He figured that because the house was completely covered with heavy tarps, he could sneak in, grab some loot, and slip out without worrying that anyone would confront him. He saw the signs posted all around the house warning of deadly chemicals inside but thought he could hold his breath while he cleaned out the place of all its valuables.

Tragically, he was wrong—dead wrong. Exterminators found his body inside the house the next day. The thief lost his life for nothing. The house was entirely empty of any possessions because the new owners hadn't moved in yet!

* * *

A very nervous robber walked into a restaurant in Newport, Rhode Island, flashed a gun, and demanded cash.

After collecting $400, he put the money in a bag and tried to stuff the bag into his shirt pocket. Stupidly, he used his gun to jam the money in his pocket. The gun went off, killing him instantly.

THE SPORTS HALL OF SHAME

SOME THINGS ARE BETTER LEFT UNSAID

Before a 1993 NBA game between the Miami Heat and the visiting Chicago Bulls, superstar Scottie Pippen sent a note to the home team's dressing room.

In the note, the Chicago forward reminded the Miami players that the Bulls had a perfect 19–0 lifetime record against the Heat. "We own you," Pippen's note boasted.

The message was designed to psych out Miami. Instead, it angered the Heat so much that they whipped the Bulls 97–95 for Miami's first-ever win against Chicago.

ONCE UPON A TIME (OUT)

With only twenty seconds left in the 1993 NCAA basketball championship, the Michigan Wolverines trailed the North Carolina Tar Heels 73–71.

After grabbing a rebound, Michigan's Chris Webber brought the ball up the court. The star had a chance to tie or win the game for the Wolverines. Instead, he helped the Tar Heels win by committing one of the greatest gaffes in college basketball history.

Webber dribbled down the right side toward the corner. Sensing that he was going to be trapped by two North Carolina players, Webber called time with only eleven seconds left.

At first, he didn't understand why the Tar Heels were jumping for joy or why his teammates were throwing their hands up in despair. But everyone, including the 64,000 fans at the New Orleans Superdome, knew why.

Michigan didn't have any time-outs remaining!

As a result, the referees called a technical foul on Webber. North Carolina's Donald Williams went to the free-throw line and sank both foul shots. When the Tar Heels got the ball again, Williams was fouled. He made both shots to cement a thrilling 77–71 victory.

Webber and his teammates were in shock after the game. "We were yelling, 'No time-out, no time-out,'" recalled Michigan's James Voskuil. For whatever reason, Webber didn't grasp that his team had no time-outs left, even though Coach Steve Fisher had told his players moments before the blunder.

"If I'd known we didn't have any time-outs, I never would have called one," Webber told reporters. "I called time-out and that probably cost us the game."

However, unlike many sports goats, Webber did not go into hiding after the screwup. He attended banquets and politely answered questions from reporters, even though it was painful for him. "You not only find out who your friends are when something like this happens, you find out you have friends you didn't even know you had," said Webber.

One of them was President Clinton, who wrote Webber shortly after the costliest time-out of all time. "Part of playing for high stakes under pressure is the constant risk of mental error," read the President's letter. "I know. I have lost two political races and made countless mistakes over the last twenty years. . . . You can always regret what occurred, but don't let it get you down or take away the satisfaction of what you have accomplished. You have a great future. Hang in there."

Webber did "hang in there." He went on to play in the NBA.

LOSING TRACK OF TIME

Playing at home against the Los Angeles Lakers, the Dallas Mavericks desperately needed a victory to even the 1984 NBA play-off series at two wins apiece.

With thirty-one seconds left and the score tied at 108, Dallas center Pat Cummings went to the free-throw line. Meanwhile, his teammate Derek Harper talked strategy with Coach Dick Motta.

After Cummings missed the foul shot, the Lakers got the rebound but failed to score. The Mavericks rebounded and hurried up the court, hoping to win with a last-second shot. Cummings passed to Harper. But to his teammates' shock, Harper dribbled the final six seconds off the clock without even trying to score.

As the buzzer sounded, Harper threw the ball up in the air in celebration, believing his team had won the game. His angry teammates pointed to the scoreboard. When Harper saw the score was still knotted at 108, his jaw dropped.

Harper's blunder sent the game into overtime, where the Lakers ripped the Mavericks 122–115 and went on to win the play-off series. "I'll take the blame for the loss," said Harper afterward. "It was a mistake. I thought Cummings made the foul shot that put us ahead."

FUNKY DUNK

University of Cincinnati guard Brian Williams made the most shameful dunk in college basketball history during a 1977 game against the University of Louisville.

Williams soared down the lane and launched himself for what looked like a dramatic jam. Meanwhile, referee Darwin Brown positioned himself under the basket.

Williams sailed high in the air, held the ball straight over his head, and slammed it down. Incredibly, he missed not only the basket but the backboard as well. In fact, he missed everything—except the referee. The ball smashed into Brown's head and bounced crazily into the seats.

"The crowd loved it," recalled the ref, "but I darn near got knocked out. I staggered around and had the same thought as everyone else: How could he miss the basket like that?"

RIGHT MOVE, WRONG TEAM

With only nine seconds left and the scoreboard reading "Home 62, Visitors 61," basketball coach Chris Cagle called a time-out during a 1968 game in the Buhl (Idaho) High gym.

The coach told his players to hold the ball and run out the clock. But when play resumed, Cagle realized he had made a terrible mistake.

Cagle had grown up in Buhl and played high-school basketball in the very same gym where the game was being held. After college, he began a teaching career at nearby Twin Falls High, the team he now coached.

When he looked at the scoreboard during the time-out,

Cagle momentarily forgot that his team was not the "home" team in his old gym. His players were the "visitors." So when he told them to stall, they followed his orders—and naturally lost the game!

THAT'S USING YOUR HEAD

During a 1993 game, Texas Rangers right fielder José Canseco found a novel way to knock a baseball over the fence—even though he wasn't at the plate.

Cleveland Indians batter Carlos Martinez lofted a deep fly ball toward right field. Canseco raced back to the wall and leaped. But he mistimed his jump. The ball landed on top of his head and bounced over the fence for a heads-up home run!

To add insult to injury, the homer proved to be the difference in the Rangers' 7–6 loss. "What can I say?" the red-faced Canseco said after the game. "I'm an entertainer."

EXCUSE ME, BUT THIS BAG BELONGS TO ME

The Baltimore Orioles looked like Little Leaguers rather than major leaguers during a 1993 game. On one shameful play, the Orioles wound up with three runners on third—at the same time!

The Orioles had loaded the bases when the batter hit a short fly ball that struck the ground a split second before it was fielded by the California Angels right fielder. Orioles runner Jeff Tackert, who had been on third base, ran halfway home and then went back to the bag, wrongly thinking the ball had been caught. But Brady Anderson, the runner on second, ran to third because he saw the ball had landed safely for a base hit. Chito Martinez, who chugged around the bases from first to third, also believed it was a hit.

All three runners met at third base, which is a no-no. Angels catcher John Orton tagged all three—and wound up with a double play when the umpire ruled that only Anderson was entitled to third base.

SOCK IT TO ME

Seattle Mariners superstar outfielder Ken Griffey, Jr., arrived at the clubhouse for a 1993 game and realized that he had the wrong pair of team socks.

He turned to his favorite Mariners coach—his father, Ken Griffey, Sr.—and swapped socks with dear old dad. However, the socks didn't come without a little embarrassment for the all-star.

In front of all the other Mariners, Senior told Junior, "After all these years, I'm still dressing you."

DON'T TAKE UP DARTS

During a 1993 major league game, Los Angeles Dodgers all-star catcher Mike Piazza tried to throw out a runner stealing second base.

Dodgers pitcher Tom Candiotti did what he always did in that kind of situation. He bent over so the catcher had a clear throw and turned toward second base.

Unfortunately, Piazza's throw never made it to the second baseman. The catcher's rifle throw accidentally nailed Candiotti square on the butt! Said the pitcher later, "I've dodged line drives before, but never a catcher's throw."

✻   ✻   ✻

While making his debut as a pro baseball pitcher for the minor league Elmira (New York) Pioneers in 1993, Florida Marlins first-round draft pick Marc Valdes was very nervous.

The young pitcher threw his first warm-up pitch so hard and wild that it sailed past the catcher—and smacked into the umpire's face. Fortunately, the ump was wearing his face mask and wasn't hurt. As for Valdes, he was aching from embarrassment.

SO WHAT'S THE BIG STINK?

Before a 1993 minor league baseball game in Ohio, a skunk ambled onto the field.

The players all fled to the safety of their dugout. But Apolinar Garcia, a pitcher for Canton-Akron, claimed he had a way with animals. He bravely walked up to the critter. To everyone's astonishment, the skunk stopped and looked at the player as Garcia bent down to pet it.

Just as Garcia was showing off his skill at making friends with wild animals, the skunk threw a big stink. No one got near Garcia for the rest of the day.

IT'S NOT OVER 'TIL IT'S OVER

With five seconds to play and his Shawnee Mission (Kansas) South High Raiders leading 24–21, quarterback Butch Ross knew his team had won. All he had to do was take the snap and fall on the ball to win the state play-off game.

It was football's simplest play. Or so it seemed.

Ross took the snap at the 40-yard line of the archrival Shawnee Mission West Vikings. He backpedaled for a few yards and happily watched the final seconds tick off. Then, in celebration, Ross started shaking teammates' hands as cheering South High fans charged onto the field.

But although there was no time left on the clock, there was still enough time for Ross to goof up. He never bothered to down the ball!

Vikings safety John Reichart was smart enough to realize that the ball was still in play because Ross's knee had yet to touch the ground. So Reichart raced up to the unsuspecting Ross, snatched the ball from him at the 25-yard line, and ran into the end zone. The officials immediately signaled a touchdown for the Vikings. Ross's blunder had turned a sure 24–21 Raiders victory into a stunning 27–24 season-ending defeat.

HE WENT THATAWAY

During a 1964 game against the San Francisco 49ers, the visiting Minnesota Vikings were winning 27–17 early in the fourth quarter.

Vikings defensive end Jim Marshall then picked up a fumble, broke into the open, and headed for the end zone. His teammates on the sidelines ran beside him stride for stride, screaming.

"I thought they were cheering for me," Marshall recalled. "About the five-yard line, I looked around and things didn't seem right." For one thing, the hometown San Francisco fans were cheering. For another thing, Vikings quarterback Fran Tarkenton, watching from the sidelines, was pointing in the opposite direction.

Marshall had run 62 yards into the wrong end zone! Instead of scoring a touchdown for his team, he had scored a two-point safety for the 49ers. Marshall didn't realize what he had done until San Francisco's Bruce Bosley thanked him for the points. "I told Jim, 'Thanks. We could use more of those,'" recalled Bosley.

"You can imagine how it was for me," Marshall said later. "I have never felt so humiliated."

His teammates forgave him because the Vikings still won the game 27–22. "On the flight back to Minnesota, they asked me to take over as the pilot," said Wrong-Way Marshall. "They figured I'd land them in Hawaii."

SILENT MIGHT

Gallaudet, the famed college for the hearing-impaired, took on a bunch of collegiate all-stars years ago in a football game.

The all-stars, known as the Norfolk Blues, were so cocky that they didn't huddle up or call signals. Instead, they talked openly about what play to run because they figured Gallaudet's deaf players couldn't hear them.

But the Norfolk Blues didn't know one important fact about their opponents. The Gallaudet players were expert lip readers! Gallaudet whipped Norfolk 20–0.

THIS SLAP STICK WASN'T FUNNY

Even a hockey superstar like Wayne Gretzky can screw up.

During a 1993 NHL game, Gretzky, then playing for the Los Angeles Kings, was in front of his team's net, trying to prevent a goal. He deflected a Montreal

Canadiens pass. But in doing so, he accidentally hit the puck past his own goalie and into the Kings' net!

"I couldn't believe it," recalled the Great One. "I wished I could have sunk through the ice because I was so embarrassed."

Fortunately, it was the only goal Montreal scored in the Kings' 4–1 victory.

KISS-UP

Randy Pierce, right wing for the NHL's Colorado Rockies, scored a goal late in the game against the New York Islanders to seal a 7–4 victory in 1979.

Pierce was so pleased with himself that he plucked the puck out of the net, kissed it, and tossed it over the safety glass and into the crowd.

His grin quickly turned to a frown when the referee gave Pierce a two-minute penalty for delay of game.

A TAIL OF WOE

Racehorse Basic Witness was a favorite to win the 1974 Longport Handicap stake race at the Atlantic City Race Track. Jockey Carlos Barrera sat poised in the saddle as the back stall door on the starting gate closed behind him.

Moments later, the front gate opened with a clang and all the horses took off—except for Basic Witness. He didn't go anywhere. Barrera gave him a kick, but all the horse would do was paw frantically at the dirt. Only then did the jockey discover why his horse wouldn't move. Basic Witness's tail was stuck in the rear door of the gate!

"No one, not even the old-timers, had ever seen anything like it," recalled track steward Sam Boulmetis. "It was a funny sight. Luckily, the horse wasn't hurt—although I'm not so sure his feelings weren't."

IT'S THE PITS!

At the 1979 Rebel 500 stock car race at Darlington Raceway, driver David Pearson pulled his Mercury into the pits.

His crack pit crew decided to change all four tires on the stop. As they worked, Pearson, who was in fourth place, kept his eyes glued to the leader, and eventual winner, Darrell Waltrip, who had also come in for a pit stop.

Pearson wrongly assumed that his crew was only changing the tires on the right side of his car. He didn't notice that when they finished with that side, the crew loosened the two left wheels. To the pitmen's complete surprise, Pearson gunned the motor.

Crewman Eddie Wood yelled, "Whoa!" But Pearson thought Wood shouted, "Go!"

Pearson drove off—but his car didn't go very far. About 50 yards (46 meters) down the pit lane, both left wheels flew off and his car came to a screeching halt. The runaway wheels bounded down pit row as wide-eyed crewmen leaped out of the way.

"Of all the things that have ever happened to me," said the veteran racer, "I can't think of anything worse."

After he got over his anger and embarrassment, Pearson laughed when a friend suggested that the driver think about "re-tiring."

UNFINISHED BUSINESS

Race-car driver Mark Martin was thrilled. He had a ten-car-length lead over his nearest opponent as he zoomed past what he thought was the finish line of the 1994 Goody's 250.

He triumphantly headed for the victory lane, thinking he had won. What he had done was pull a major blunder. To everyone's shock, Martin had mistakenly driven off the track just 300 yards (275 meters) away from the finish line.

As Martin was celebrating, driver David Green took the checkered flag. Moments later, Martin realized he had lost because he failed to finish the final lap. "I thought it was over," he told reporters. "It was the dumbest thing I've ever done in my life."

LOOK, MA! NO SKIS!

Chuck Ryan hadn't planned on it, but he set the unofficial record for the longest ski jump—without skis!

More than 2,500 fans were on hand during the 1959 Duluth Invitational ski jumping championships in Fond du Lac, Minnesota. Ryan, a nine-year veteran with the St. Paul Ski Club, put on new skis but failed to test the bindings that held the skis to his ski boots.

When he hit the takeoff of the 60-meter slide, both of Ryan's skis flew off his feet. As he soared through the air for 148 feet (45 meters), Ryan told himself to prepare for a rough landing. He hit the snow at an angle and skidded another 100 feet (31 meters) before coming to a stop, unhurt.

"I just jumped out of my skis," he recalled. "I wasn't really scared, but I kept thinking that I'd better not land on my feet and risk breaking my legs. So I went in like a baseball player sliding into second."

GAME, SET, SPLASH

Before Hank Pfister was a world-ranked tennis pro, he was a Junior Davis Cup player who competed in the 1976 National 21-and-Unders tournament held in New York City.

Pfister made it to the finals, where he won the first two sets but then dropped the next two. When he lost his serve in the first game of the final set, Pfister was so ticked off at himself that he threw his tennis racquet into the air. But he tossed it a little too hard. The racquet flew over the fence and into the East River, which flowed beside the court.

"Even though there were about 1,500 people in the stands, I halted play and went after my racquet," Pfister said. "At the edge of the water, I tried to reach out for the racquet, but I missed. The current was carrying it farther down the river. I took one more step into the water—and went straight down, totally under water! When I got back to the surface, I grabbed my racquet and swam back to shore.

"The East River is not exactly clean. When I returned to the court, I was dripping wet and had green gunk hanging all over me. The crowd went nuts laughing."

Pfister resumed play—and lost the set and the match.

"It definitely was shameful," he said. "But now as I look back on the whole thing, it sure was funny."

MEDAL OF DISHONOR

Of all the athletes who ever won an Olympic gold medal, none screwed up the presentation more shamefully than Vyacheslav Ivanov. He managed to lose his hard-earned medal just seconds after receiving it!

At the 1956 Olympics in Melbourne, Australia, Ivanov, an eighteen-year-old Russian, was competing in the single sculls (a narrow, racing rowboat) on Lake Wendouree. Although no one expected him to do well, he beat out the two favorites and finished first.

Ivanov was thrilled beyond belief. He clapped his hands and shouted with joy as he and the other medalists climbed onto a float tied to the dock for the awards ceremony. When he was given his gold medal, Ivanov jumped up and down with glee. But in his happiness, he accidentally dropped the medal. It fell right between two of the float's wooden slats and sank to the muddy bottom of the lake.

The horrified teen jumped into the water and tried to find his lost medal. After repeated dives into the 5-foot-deep (1.5-meter) lake, the crushed Ivanov gave up. The next day, about three hundred Australian school children searched the underwater reeds and muddy bottom but failed to find it.

The Olympic Committee gave Ivanov another gold medal. But he never lived down the fact that he had lost his medallion just seconds after receiving it.

WHAT A KNOCK OUT!

Boxer Henry Wallitsch was knocked out by his own worst enemy—himself!

It happened during a 1959 heavyweight fight on Long

Island, New York, against Bartolo Soni.

In the third round, Wallitsch took a wild swing that hit nothing but air. The force of his missed punch made him lose his balance, and he fell through the ropes headfirst. His chin hit the floor so hard that it knocked him out.

Even though Soni never landed a punch in the round, the record books show that he knocked out Wallitsch. But in truth, Wallitsch was the one who knocked out Wallitsch.

AT LEAST HE AIMED HIGH

The wildest ball ever thrown in a pro bowling tournament wasn't a gutter ball. It was a ceiling ball!

It happened during the 1971 Cougar Open at the Madison Square Garden Bowling Center. Palmer Fallgren, who was in his second year on the pro bowling tour, had just thrown a 4–6 split—an almost impossible situation in which two remaining pins are on the opposite sides of the lane.

"I was so angry, I didn't wait for my ball to get back," Fallgren recalled. "I had another ball, so I just grabbed it and threw it as hard as I could."

In his haste and fury, Fallgren forgot about the tape he had placed in the finger holes of his spare ball before the tournament. When he tried to release the ball on his follow-through, it stuck to his fingers for a second. Instead of rolling the ball straight down the alley, Fallgren launched it straight up!

The 16-pound (7.25-kilogram) ball smashed into the 15-foot-high (4.6-meter) ceiling. Then it fell to the alley with a loud bang about 10 feet (30 meters) in front of the foul line. Finally the ball rolled down the lane—and knocked down the 4 pin.

"I went into total shock," Fallgren recalled. "It was so embarrassing. I didn't know what to say or do. When the ball hit the floor, it sounded like a cannonball and the bowlers on the other lanes just stopped right in their tracks. I was frozen, too, just staring at the ceiling. I couldn't believe what I had done."

Said Tom Roballey, director of the bowling center, "He dented not only the ceiling but the lane as well. We had to put down new wood.

"It could have been a lot worse. When Fallgren's ball hit the ceiling, it missed a sprinkler head [which turns on in case of fire] by just three inches (8 centimeters). If the ball had struck it, we would have been flooded."

STUCK IN THE GUTTER

During one horrendous night, Richard Caplette set the American Bowling Congress record for the lowest score in league play—an incredible 3! Not only that, but he also established a black mark for the most gutter balls in a single game.

Caplette was not a terrible bowler. He owned a respectable scoring average of 170. But not on this night in 1971!

"No matter what I tried, I just couldn't keep the ball on the alley," recalled Caplette, of Danielson, Connecticut.

He knocked down only three pins on his first ball. Little did he know that those would be the only pins he would hit for the rest of the game.

"I couldn't stop throwing gutter balls," he said. "I was

really trying my best too. Our scores were posted overhead and that didn't help. After each gutter ball, someone would come over and say, 'Can I help you?'"

Apparently, no one could. Caplette finished by throwing a league record nineteen straight gutter balls.

"I completely gave up bowling after that," he said. "I never threw another ball. I was too embarrassed to show my face around an alley again."

THAT'S THE WAY THE BALL BOUNCES

Golf may look like a quiet, safe sport. But sometimes it can get downright dangerous. For example:

• Amateur golfer Bill Thomas scored a "hole in three" on one wild shot. In 1991, at the Salishan Golf Course in Gleneden Beach, Oregon, Thomas sliced his drive onto Highway 101 and nailed three moving vehicles. The ball broke the windshield of a car, then bounced into the windshield of a pickup, and finally slammed into the back of another truck. No one was hurt, and the damage was covered by insurance.

• Faye Shelbourne was using her grandmother's antique clubs during a 1988 round of golf in Victoria, British Columbia, Canada. As she went into her backswing, the clubhead flew off and smashed a window in the pro shop.

• In 1963, Jim Armstrong, of Phoenix, Arizona, was playing at the Desert Forest Golf Club in Carefree, Arizona. His tee shot on the second hole hit a tee marker and rebounded straight back, striking him in the head.

When Armstrong recovered a few minutes later, he tried another tee shot. Incredibly, it hit the same marker! This time, the ball flew back and smacked him in the knee. That was enough pain for one day. Armstrong limped off the course.

THE WHEEL OF MISFORTUNE

DINNER WAS A REAL BLAST

Christmas dinner turned into an awful mess for Chris Lee. He accidentally blew up the turkey!

In 1996, Lee, of Halifax, West Yorkshire, England, had invited eight friends and family members over for a holiday supper. "It was a big mistake," he later admitted.

After shoving stuffing into the huge 22-pound (10-kilogram) turkey, Lee put it in the oven and went into the next room to entertain his guests. When he looked at his wrist to check the time, he realized that his watch was missing. He thought he had left it at his girlfriend's house.

Lee was wrong. His watch had slipped off his wrist when he was stuffing the turkey. The cooking bird now had a time bomb inside it because the battery in Lee's watch expanded as the oven heated up. Eventually, the watch exploded, hurling the turkey through the oven door and rocking the house with a deafening blast.

"It frightened the life out of me," Lee recalled. "The

kitchen was a scene of devastation. I couldn't believe my eyes." He had to scrape pieces of turkey off the walls and ceiling. "It took me hours to clean everything up." His pet Labrador, Zoe, helped by lapping up turkey bits that had been hurled onto the floor.

So what did Lee do for Christmas dinner? He served his guests chicken pizza.

"Fortunately, they saw the funny side and treated it as a joke, though I wasn't laughing. Next year I'm definitely going out for Christmas dinner."

AN EXPENSIVE DISH

In 1993, Jane Butlin of Paignton, England, wanted to make an extra-special dinner for her boyfriend. Knowing how much he liked vegetables, she prepared some brussels sprouts and cooked them in the oven.

When her boyfriend arrived and learned what she had done, he was not happy. It wasn't that he had anything against brussels sprouts. He was upset because Jane had forgotten that he had stashed £3,000 ($4,700) in cash in her oven for safekeeping. All the cash had turned to ash.

NEXT TIME, HIRE SOMEONE

Clancy Fegan and his wife, Mandy, decided that they didn't want to pay lots of money to remodel their house in Cardiff, Wales. They figured they could do it themselves.

So, in 1996, Clancy tore down several inside walls to make a larger room. When the not-so-handy man noticed cracks appearing in the remaining walls, he went to the building-supply store for some plaster.

He need not have bothered. When he returned home, he discovered he had a much bigger problem. The walls were no longer cracked. In fact, the walls were no longer there. They had collapsed, causing his entire house to fall down.

SOAKING IT UP

Kay Cox was trying to be a good mom by letting her two-year-old daughter, Georgia, play with the hose in their backyard in London, England.

Georgia was having a wonderful time watering the flowers and grass. When the doorbell rang, Kay hurried to the front door, leaving Georgia alone on the lawn.

Meanwhile, having watered everything in the backyard, Georgia was looking for other things to spray. She dragged the hose into the house—and began drenching the furniture, carpet, and curtains in the living room. By the time Cox discovered what the little girl was doing, the room had been soaked, causing thousands of dollars in damage.

Cox vowed never to let Georgia play with the hose again.

CLEANED OUT

Robert Keeler of Harrisburg, Pennsylvania, used his shop vacuum to suck gasoline out of the tank of his car in 1994.

That wasn't a smart idea. Sparks from the vacuum ignited the gasoline, causing an explosion that sent flames shooting 30 feet (9 meters) into the air.

The good news was that Keeler wasn't hurt. The bad news was that his car was destroyed—and so was his newly remodeled $200,000 house.

IT CAME OUT IN THE WASH

Al and Pat Sutton were lottery winners one day and losers the next.

The Suttons, of Rapid City, South Dakota, were visiting relatives in Richland Hills, Texas, for Thanksgiving in 1996 when Al bought one hundred lottery tickets. He hoped one of them would hit the $50 million jackpot.

"We've got a winner!" he shouted when he saw five of the six winning numbers on one of his tickets. The ticket was worth $1,923.

Al kept the ticket in his shirt pocket. The next morning, while Al took a shower, Pat did the laundry. "I put a load of clothes in the washing machine, then I went into the bedroom and saw his shirt," she recalled. She tossed the shirt into the wash, forgetting to check the pocket.

When Al stepped out of the shower, he immediately noticed his shirt was gone. After Al shouted to Pat, the couple bolted for the washing machine and peered inside. Recalled Pat, "We saw these little, tiny bits of paper. I said, 'Oh, my goodness!' I was very upset. Tears were rolling."

Said Al, as he watched the remains of his $1,923 ticket swirl in the washer, "There's nothing we can do about it now. It's just one of those things."

THIS COULD NEVER HAPPEN TO YOUR MOM, COULD IT?

The next time your mom gets upset with you because you have left the house a mess, ask her to read the following story. It came from the Internet and was written by a mother of six kids who is known in cyberspace as MOM x SIX. She says:

"My oldest two kids (nine and seven) accidentally called 911 and hung up. Then they panicked. They ran to my neighbor's house, where I was with the rest of my crew. But the two kids didn't tell me of the call they had made— or that they had left the back door wide open.

"The phone rang at the neighbor's where I was. It was from a friend, who said she had called my house and a policeman had answered the phone.

"I ran home to find several squad cars in the front and policemen in my house. It seems that when the responding officer arrived to do the routine check for 911 hang-ups, he found the back door open and went inside. He found what appeared to be a ransacked house. All the cushions were off the couch and chairs (the kids were building a fort), clothes were strewn everywhere (it was laundry day), dishes were scattered throughout the house (my husband was out of town so I was taking time off).

"The police determined that I had a lot of kids, no maid, and little ambition that day. The police thought it was so funny (I was red from embarrassment) that they didn't even lecture the kids about calling 911. (I guess they figured the kids would get lectured enough by me.)

"After I tearfully told my husband what had happened, he thought I should call a maid service to come over. We wondered if the Department of Children and Family Services had been called by the police.

"Ah, the joy of kids. I do try to keep up better now, by the way."

A NEW MEANING FOR POTTY TRAINING

While on board a high-speed train from Paris to Toulouse, France, in 1994, a passenger accidentally dropped his wallet in the toilet.

He reached down to grab it, but somehow he ended up with his hand stuck in the toilet bowl. No matter how hard he tried, he couldn't free himself. He managed to push the emergency alarm, which brought the train to a halt.

Rescue workers were brought in, but they couldn't get his hand out of the toilet. They spent two hours cutting the toilet out of the floor, then took the man to the hospital with the toilet bowl still stuck to his hand. It took doctors another hour to finally free the man from the toilet bowl.

WRECKING BALLS

Bowling balls don't roll only down the alley. They've been known to take some strange paths that have caused trouble for their owners. For example:

• In 1960, Louie Montesi of Memphis, Tennessee, had just purchased a new ball and was driving to the bowling center to try it out for the first time. Stopping for a red light, Montesi heard a thump and then an "uh-oh" from his thirteen-year-old son in the backseat.

The boy had been playing with the ball when he accidentally pitched it out the open window—just as the car was at the top of a hill. As the ball rolled merrily down the street, cars swerved to avoid the runaway object. The ball wound up in a sewer drain two blocks away. Now that was a gutter ball!

• In 1976, William R. Williams of Wilkes-Barre, Pennsylvania, was driving his car when he hit the brakes a little too hard. His bowling ball, which was by his side, rolled off the front seat and dropped onto the gas pedal.

The car sped up, startling Williams so much that he lost control of his vehicle. His auto crashed into a parked car and pushed it into another parked vehicle. Luckily, no one was hurt.

• In Syracuse, New York, in 1958, a woman bowler boarded a bus headed for the bowling center. She placed her bowling bag, which had a broken zipper and wouldn't close, on the floor.

Moments later, a traffic light turned red and the bus driver slammed on the brakes. The sudden stop caused the bowling bag to tip over. The ball rolled out of the bag and down the aisle.

A passenger took one look at the ball and shouted, "It's a bomb! Run!" The other passengers screamed in panic and dashed off the bus before the embarrassed bowler had a chance to tell everyone the "bomb" was just a bowling ball.

NOT TOO THMART, THONNY

On one of the coldest days of 1996 in Glenwood Springs, Colorado, nine-year-old Hunter Cunningham was playing with a friend, who urged him to try an experiment.

"Why don't you find out what happens when you touch a metal pole with your tongue," said the friend.

Hunter found out. His wet tongue stuck to the frozen pole, and he needed help from firefighters to get freed. Hunter's face wound up as red as his sore tongue.

SHUT-EYE

In Bangkok, Thailand, in 1996, Panarat Tangpratum wanted to soothe her stinging eyes after a hard day of selling oranges at an outdoor market. The forty-two-year-old woman went into the bathroom to use eyewash.

Grabbing the small bottle, she put a few drops in her eyes. But instead of finding relief, she found that she couldn't see. In fact, she couldn't even open her eyes.

After being taken to the hospital, Tangpratum learned that what she had thought was eyewash was really glue! Doctors managed to flush the glue out of her eyes with water and oil. Her sight immediately returned to normal.

Said the embarrassed woman, "I should have read the label."

DROPPING OFF TO SLEEP

A thirty-seven-year-old man was hiking with three friends in England in 1997 when they set up camp on the top of a cliff on the North Yorkshire coast.

Later that night, the man placed his sleeping bag near the edge of the cliff and snuggled in. The next morning, his companions woke up to discover that he was missing. They searched everywhere but failed to find him or his sleeping bag.

But then one of the campers looked over the edge

of the cliff. To his horror, he found his friend—70 feet (21 meters) below, at the base of the cliff. The missing man had rolled over in his sleep and plunged down the cliff.

Incredibly, he wasn't seriously injured. "He is lucky to be alive," said a police spokesman. "The only reason he wasn't killed is that he was asleep at the time he fell."

✳ ✳ ✳

Ian Smith, thirty-four, dreamed he was hanging onto the ledge of a seaside cliff—and woke up to find it was true.

It happened in 1996 after Smith went to bed at an inn near Devon, England. While experiencing a vivid dream, he walked in his sleep from his hotel room to the beach half a mile (.8 kilometer) away. Then, while still sleeping, he began climbing the cliff. He awakened about 2:30 A.M., 40 feet (12 meters) above the rocky shore, clinging to the ledge for dear life.

Smith began shouting for help, but it took nearly an hour before a woman who lived nearby heard him. She went to investigate and, after discovering Smith's plight, called rescuers. They used ropes to get him off the ledge.

Joked one of his rescuers, "I hope you don't sleep near any tall buildings."

WHEN LIFE IMITATES ART

Scottish author Dougal Haston had spent months working tirelessly on his novel. When it was finally finished, he treated himself to a vacation.

He decided to go to Leysin, Switzerland—the same place where the main character in Haston's novel became a victim of an avalanche while skiing.

Incredibly, just like the character in his novel, Haston was caught in an avalanche while skiing. In his book, the character survived. However, in real life, Haston didn't.

EXPLOSIVE PERSONALITIES

Paul Stiller and his wife, Bonnie, of Andover Township, New Jersey, were driving around town one night in 1996, bored out of their minds.

They had a quarter stick of dynamite in their car. One of them got the terrible idea to light it and toss it out the window to see what would happen. So they lit the stick and threw it. What the Stillers failed to realize—until it was too late—was that they had forgotten to roll down the window!

Needless to say, the car blew up. The Stillers were lucky to escape with minor injuries.

FIRED-UP FANS

Soccer fans in the village of Ixiamas, Bolivia, celebrated too hard in 1993 when their national soccer team won a qualifying match in the World Cup.

The fans shot off fireworks in the middle of town. Unfortunately, the burning embers from the fireworks fell directly onto their huts. The flaming debris set the fans' homes on fire and burned down most of the village.

THE HUNTER BECOMES THE HUNTED

In 1993, Steven Reynolds of Arlington, Virginia, went hunting for wild turkey.

He crouched down in the tall grass and blew into a whistle-like device that imitated the call of a turkey, hoping it would lure the wild bird. It didn't. What it did attract was a hungry bobcat, which sneaked up from behind and attacked Reynolds—because it mistook *him* for a wild turkey.

WELL, EXCUUUUSE ME!

When a driver gets into an accident, he files a claim with his insurance company, which usually helps pay for any damages. Here are some wacky excuses from drivers, taken from actual claim forms and published in the *Toronto Sun*:

• Coming home, I drove into the wrong driveway and collided with a tree I don't have.

• The other car collided with mine without giving warning of its intentions.

• The pedestrian [a person who is walking] had no idea which way to run, so I ran over him.

• The driver was all over the road; I had to swerve a number of times before I hit [his car].

• In my attempt to kill a fly, I drove into a telephone pole.

• An invisible car came out of nowhere, struck my car, and vanished.

• I thought my window was down, but I found out that it was up when I put my head through it.

• I was thrown from the car as it left the road. I was later found in a ditch by some stray cows.

• The telephone pole was approaching. I was attempting to swerve out of its way when it struck the front end.

BAD VIBRATIONS

When a mysterious ticking sound was heard coming from a suitcase at the train station in Springfield, Massachusetts, in 1996, officials became suspicious.

They carefully examined the piece of luggage, which was in a storage area. The bag had been checked in advance by a passenger traveling to Atlanta. Employees tried to call the phone number listed on the baggage tag, but the number had been disconnected.

Fearing the worst—that the suitcase contained a bomb—officials called police, who ordered everyone out of the building.

Officers carefully opened the suitcase. Fortunately, they didn't find a bomb. What they did find was a battery-operated vibrating massager in the "on" position. The owner soon arrived—then quickly left town.

GUNNING FOR TROUBLE

One of the first rules that any person learns about cleaning a gun is to make sure it's empty.

A thirty-eight-year-old man from Princeton, West Virginia, forgot that lesson. While he was cleaning his .32-caliber handgun in 1992, it went off, nicking him in the right foot.

Deciding that the wound wasn't bad because it didn't hurt very much, the man began cleaning a different weapon, a .389-caliber pistol. Once again, he failed to check if it was empty—and once again, he accidentally shot himself in the same foot.

The second bullet "stung a little, but not too bad," he later told authorities. So the man took out his .357-caliber pistol, failing to see if it was loaded. It was. Incredibly, this gun too went off—and shot him in the right foot!

The man finally decided to call an ambulance. Meanwhile, friends tried to convince him to give up his gun collection.

✸ ✸ ✸

When it came to guns, police officer Randy Youngman was a stickler for safety. No matter where he went in the town of Medicine Hat, Alberta, Canada, he preached gun safety.

During a firearms safety course in 1996, Youngman was demonstrating how to safely load and unload a 12-gauge shotgun. Imagine how painfully embarrassed he was when he accidentally shot himself in the leg.

TROUBLE SLEEPING

Sari Zayed, a thirty-one-year-old woman from Davis, California, liked to sleep with her window open. That caused trouble for her in 1994.

The problem was that she snored—not faint snorts, but ear-shattering, foghorn-like blasts. Her loud snoring kept neighbors awake at night.

In fact, Zayed's snoring was so bad, she was ticketed by police! They said she violated a city ordinance banning any sound that disturbs the peace.

WHAT'S ONE VOTE?

Herb Connolly learned firsthand that every vote counts. In a 1988 election, he lost by a single vote—because he didn't vote!

Connolly ran for reelection to the Governor's Council in Massachusetts—a seat he had held for twenty years. "Normally, I voted the first thing in the morning," he recalled. "But because I had just flown in from Alaska the night before, I slept a tad longer than usual.

"Then I went right to campaign headquarters to get my workers to make calls urging people to vote. I knew it was going to be a close race.

"Early that evening I realized I hadn't voted yet. I looked at my watch. It was 7:45 P.M. I had only fifteen minutes to get to the polls." His voting place, a grade school, was about fifteen minutes away.

He arrived at 8:02 P.M. "I thought I could still get in and vote, but the doors were locked," he said. "It reminded me of those days in school when you arrive late for class and you have that terrible sinking feeling.

"I waited outside, hoping that when one of the voters opened the door, I would slip in and try to vote. About 8:05, the door opened and out stepped a friend. I went to grab for the door handle, but my friend thought I was reaching out to shake his hand. He grabbed my hand, shook it, and said, 'Herb, I voted for you.' By then, the door had slammed shut again and locked.

"By the time the next person came out, it was much too late for me to vote, so I walked away. I never thought I would lose by one vote. But I did—mine."

A BRIEF PROBLEM

Alabama senator Howell Heflin was in a serious discussion during a Senate committee hearing in 1994.

Stopping to mop his sweaty forehead, he reached into

his pocket to pull out his handkerchief. Imagine his shock when he pulled out a pair of his wife's underwear!

While rushing to get ready earlier that morning, Heflin had stuffed the undies in his pocket, mistakenly assuming it was a hanky.

GOLLYWOOD GOOFS

CRUISE-ING FOR TROUBLE

Tom Cruise did much of his own stunt driving in the racing movie *Days of Thunder*.

During one scene, Cruise had his lines taped to the dashboard as he zoomed around the track. He took his eyes off the road for a split second to look at his "cheat sheet," then lost control of the car and skidded into a concrete wall. Fortunately, the star wasn't hurt—just embarrassed.

SHUTTER BUGGED

Sylvester Stallone takes pride in doing most of his own stunts, but there was one time when he was too good.

During filming of the action adventure movie *Rambo III*, Sly was supposed to shoot a crossbow directly toward the camera, which was hidden behind a plywood cage. With the lens peeking out from a tiny hole cut in the wood, Stallone aimed for a masking tape "X" that was about a foot above the camera.

Although they knew Stallone was a good shot, no one

in the crew expected him to hit the "X." He didn't. From 75 yards (68.5 meters) away, Sly let fly. The arrow landed dead center, right on the $20,000—and now broken—lens!

MAKING A SPLASH

Goldie Hawn wanted to make a good impression when she was at a 1992 dinner party that included President George Bush and Hollywood celebrities.

"I was seated between Sylvester Stallone and President Bush," the actress recalled. "I was trying to act very cool. But as I was talking, I accidentally knocked over my wine glass. I splattered wine all over Sly Stallone's white tuxedo."

She said she was mortified by the mishap, but both President Bush and Sly laughed. "I had just ruined Sly's tuxedo," said Goldie. "But he was very charming about it.

"Mr. Bush laughed hysterically. Then he said to me, 'Well, Goldie, I'd ask you to pass the salt, but I'm not sure what would happen.'"

GETTING EVEN

One of Mel Gibson's sons got sweet revenge when his movie star dad was kidding him at a restaurant.

"I was teasing my son and embarrassing him, and he decided to teach me a lesson," Gibson recalled. "He got up and started tap dancing on the table. Then he shouted, 'Hey, ladies! Here's my dad! His name is Mel Gibson! Come on over!'

"I was the one who became really embarrassed," said the superstar. "It was the last time I showed up at that restaurant."

V_NN_ WH_T_'S M_ST _MB_RR_SS_NG M_M_NT

During a *Wheel of Fortune* taping in front of a live audience, Vanna White's world went topsy-turvy.

Vanna was twisting and turning letters in a slinky strapless dress when suddenly . . . *RRRIIIPPP!* Her zipper broke open all the way down her back. Vanna gasped and grabbed the front of her dress before it fell. She raced offstage and coolly returned moments later—wearing a new dress—to an enthusiastic ovation.

A CAR-AZY CAPER

Actress Michelle Pfeiffer was in the studio parking lot, trying to open a car door with her key. But the key wouldn't work. Frustrated, she took off her shoe and used it to beat on the window.

She stopped when a studio executive walked up and demanded to know why she was hitting his car. The actress suddenly realized that she had confused her car with his, because both were the same make, model, color, and year.

After stammering apologies, the flustered actress autographed her shoe and gave it to the executive—then stumbled off to find *her* car.

THE PRICE IS WRONG

Some of the zaniest moments on the popular TV game show *The Price Is Right* were accidents.

One time, a model was sitting at the wheel of a car being offered as a prize. As crew members pushed it from behind, the car smashed through a wall on the set. The camera caught the bedlam, as well as host Bob Barker ducking for cover when the wall tumbled down. "But the model never lost her stage presence," he recalled. "The car kept rolling, and she continued smiling and waving."

Another time, a contestant was supposed to turn a big wooden key to collect his prizes, but the key got stuck. Barker, a karate expert, gave the key a hard kick—and broke it.

A large woman once went into a frenzy on the show after winning a prize. "In her excitement, she chased me across the stage, picked me up in a bear hug and squeezed me so hard that she injured my ribs," Barker recalled. "Now when contestants try to corner me or give me a big hug, I dodge them."

A KNOCK-OUT ACTOR

Paul Michael Valley, who plays Ryan on the TV soap opera *Another World*, was knocked out of his world while taping what should have been a simple scene.

Valley was supposed to slump back onto a sofa, but he wasn't standing in the right spot. He missed the couch and toppled over backward. Valley banged his head on the floor hard enough to knock him out for several minutes.

When he recovered, the actor was woozy, so he was whisked to a hospital emergency room. The accident was embarrassing, but what happened next was outrageous.

A fan recognized Valley lying on a stretcher—and demanded his autograph! Recalled the actor, "This woman comes up to me and says, 'I know this is a bad time . . .' Then she hands me a pen!" Being a nice guy, Valley signed.

WIGGED OUT

Actress Ann-Margaret was dancing onstage in Las Vegas when her wig flew off—right into the orchestra pit.

"I'm a firm believer . . . that the show must go on," she recalled. "So I kept dancing—with my hair in tight pin curls.

"Finally, two chorus boys danced me [offstage], where my agonized hairdresser waited with another wig. Then I danced back onstage again to huge applause. Talk about embarrassing!"

FLIPPED OUT

Entertainer Marie Osmond was traveling on a plane when she got into a struggle with her seat. After being served a meal, she wanted to lean back. But the seat refused to budge from its upright position.

"I gave it a few vigorous thumps and bangs," she recalled. "All at once, it gave way, shooting backward with such force that it knocked all the food—not to mention the coffee—off the lunch tray of the man behind me and into his lap.

"Some of his meal even landed on the woman sitting next to him. Ordinarily, I love being in the spotlight. But I didn't enjoy the attention I got from these two."

✳ ✳ ✳

Years earlier, when Marie and her brother, Donnie, were kids, they got into trouble while playing pirates.

"We needed treasure," she recalled. "So we got Mom's jewelry box and buried it in our garden. When we finished playing, we went on to something else.

"That night, when Mom went to get her necklace, there

was no box. We finally confessed. But then we forgot where we had buried the 'treasure.' In the dark, my father and brothers started digging up the backyard. They dug through the night and into the morning before the box finally turned up."

SPLIT PERSONALITY

Actor Ernest Borgnine, who these days plays the doorman on TV's *The Single Guy*, suffered his most embarrassing moment early in his acting career.

"I played the part of a spear carrier in Shakespeare's *Much Ado About Nothing*," Borgnine recalled. "It was opening night, and there was a full house."

In one scene, the spear carriers, costumed in tights and hats, were supposed to run onstage and fall to the ground. Everything was rehearsed, including the timing of the fall. But the lead spear carrier slipped and fell too early.

"We all toppled on top of each other," the actor recalled. "I felt one leg shoot out from under me in one direction, and the other leg went the other way. Then I heard a ripping sound, and I knew what had happened without even looking. My tights had split open!

"Still on the floor, I glanced down and breathed a sigh of relief. I could see only a very small split up the front. I figured I could finish the scene without anyone noticing. Since the rip was in the front, I thought if I kept my back to the audience, I'd be okay.

"But as I kept my back to them and shuffled offstage, I heard the audience howling with laughter. I had no idea what they were laughing at.

"As soon as I got behind the curtain, I realized that my tights had split wide open and my whole fanny was showing! I'll never forget that moment for as long as I live."

SKATING ON THIN ICE

Nancy Kerrigan, winner of the 1994 Olympic silver medal in figure skating, found herself on thin ice during a parade at Disney World.

As she stood with Mickey Mouse on a float that was motoring down Main Street, Nancy told the Disney mascot her real feelings about the event: "This is so corny. This is so dumb. I hate it. This is the most corny thing I've ever done."

What she didn't realize was that her comments were picked up by television cameras filming the parade. Her slam aired on the news across the nation.

OH, JOHNNY!

For years, Johnny Carson made millions of late-night viewers laugh with his jokes on *The Tonight Show Starring Johnny Carson*. But sometimes he got his biggest laughs unintentionally.

Introducing his guests one evening, Johnny said, "And on our show tonight, we have five Miss America contestants and also some dogs. . . ." The audience burst out laughing. "I mean real dogs. . . ." The laughter got even louder. "Come on, you know I mean dogs that bark!"

✳ ✳ ✳

In 1973, Carson said, "Have you heard the latest? I'm not kidding. I saw it in the paper. There's a shortage of toilet paper."

Actually, what Carson had read was that a government official was concerned about a toilet paper shortage even though the stores were well-stocked. But for millions of viewers—and shoppers—Carson triggered "what may go down in history as one of the nation's most unusual crises," according to *The New York Times*.

Carson had unwittingly started a nationwide buying panic for toilet paper! Millions of Americans stripped every roll of bathroom tissue from thousands of grocery shelves. Thanks to his comment, there really was a toilet paper shortage. It took two weeks for the panic to end.

THE WHOLE TOOTH AND NOTHING BUT THE TOOTH

Angela Lansbury, famous for her role as Jessica Fletcher in the hit TV series *Murder, She Wrote,* was performing on Broadway in the musical *Sweeney Todd.*

During the first act, the actress was in the middle of a song when she felt a temporary front tooth loosen. Before she could do anything about it, the tooth flew out of her mouth, over the footlights, and into the front row, where it barely missed hitting a man.

"For one terrible moment, time stood still," the actress recalled. "There I was with a gap in my mouth where the tooth once was. I'd never been so embarrassed in all my life. For the rest of the song, I had to hide the gap and sing through the side of my mouth. It was simply awful.

"They say that in the face of such mishaps, one should 'grin and bear it.' But at the time, grinning wasn't the best thing to do."

WILD (AND WACKY) KINGDOM

A PURR-FECTLY AWFUL ORDEAL

When nature called, Ginette Turner-Dupuis made her way to the bathroom in her home in Aldershot, Hampshire, England, one morning in 1996. On her way, the seventy-year-old woman lovingly patted her two cats.

Had she known what was about to happen, she probably would have shooed them away instead.

Moments after Turner-Dupuis entered the bathroom and closed the door, she heard a terrible crash. When she tried to open the door, she discovered that something outside was blocking it. No amount of pushing or shoving could get the door to budge.

Turner-Dupuis could hear her cats meowing. It didn't take her long to figure out what had happened. The cats had jumped up onto a rickety cupboard that stood in the hallway right outside the bathroom door. The cupboard had fallen over, blocking the door.

Adding to the elderly woman's woes, the only window in the bathroom didn't open. She remained stuck in there for six long hours, hoping that a friend or family member would come into the unlocked house and discover her plight. But no one came.

Turner-Dupuis finally took matters into her own hands. She took off her shoe, used it to break the window, and called for help. A neighbor soon came to her rescue. The cupboard was moved to a different location. As for her cats, well, all was forgiven.

NO PUSSYFOOTING AROUND!

A judge curbed a mischief-making pet cat—by placing him under house arrest!

The roving rascal, an orange-and-white cat named Mortimer, was barred from the outdoors in 1989. It happened after his owner's neighbors in Calgary, Alberta, Canada, filed a lawsuit for damages they claimed the tiny terror had caused to their property.

The trouble started in 1983 when Al and Ann Marshall moved into the neighborhood where Mortimer lived with his owner, Garry Huskinson.

"Mortimer made our lives miserable," Mrs. Marshall recalled. "He dug up the vegetables in our garden, used our potted plants for a litter box, and even climbed through windows into our house."

One year, according to the lawsuit, Mortimer ruined the Marshalls' Easter dinner. "He managed to get into the house, and we found him munching on ham with potato salad, and pie all over the floor," said Mrs. Marshall.

"My husband suffers from asthma and I'm allergic to cats, so we had to go to the hospital after our house was invaded. We found balls of his orange and white hair under our beds."

In 1988, the Marshalls became so fed up with Mortimer that they had him picked up by the local animal shelter. Then they complained to Huskinson. "I was shocked," he said. "I knew Mortimer was a roamer, but I had no idea he was causing this kind of problem."

The following spring Huskinson received another shock when the Marshalls filed a $30,000 lawsuit against him, claiming the cat had caused damage to their property. Before the case went to trial, the judge put Mortimer under house arrest. Huskinson was ordered to keep the cat indoors except for an occasional walk—on a leash.

Eventually the lawsuit was settled. However, Mortimer's roaming days were over.

THE CAT BURGLARS

Wendy Singleton let her cat, Attila, out at night to roam the neighborhood in Chard, Somerset, England. But soon the neighbors began complaining.

It seems that Attila had developed a strange taste for cuddly toys. At night he would sneak through the cat doors of neighbors' houses and hunt for stuffed toys. If he found one, he would carry it home and add it to his collection.

By 1997, Attila had swiped more than a dozen stuffed animals, including a pink elephant that was 12 inches (30 centimeters) high. "He must have had a real struggle to get that through the cat flap," said Wendy.

✳ ✳ ✳

Then there is the case of Maurice, a cat in Wellington, New Zealand. He was caught stealing neighbors' underwear! In 1996, he brought home over sixty pairs of men's and women's undies.

His owner said she washed and folded all the stolen underwear, but no one came forward to claim any of it.

ATTACK CAT

In 1992, Bonni Matheson of Davenport, Washington, led support for a local law calling for the licensing of pet cats. Apparently, one cat didn't appreciate Mrs. Matheson's stand on the issue.

A month before the council was to vote on the proposed law, Mrs. Matheson was working in her yard, minding her own business, when suddenly a white cat showed up. It bit and clawed her hands so badly, she required treatment at the hospital.

The cat was captured and taken to the local pound for a ten-day rabies observation. But two days later, the cat escaped—and, incredibly, made its way right back to the Matheson house!

Somehow the vengeful cat sneaked inside the house, then tore up the wallpaper in the kitchen and attacked the family's three dogs in the living room. "My house was a total wreck," recalled Mrs. Matheson. "The kids and I got out of there so fast it was unbelievable."

The cat never bothered them again. But, said Mrs. Matheson, "I had a nightmare that the cat rang my doorbell, and when I opened it, the cat said, 'I'm baaack!'"

(By the way, the city council voted against the cat licensing law.)

THIS ENGINE REALLY PURRS

Buttons the cat was looking for a quiet place to nap. Instead she wound up on a wild 300-mile (483-kilometer) ride—under the hood of a car!

In 1983, the black cat ambled underneath a car owned by neighbor Fraser Robertson of Great Yarmouth, England. Buttons then climbed onto the engine. She was napping under the hood when Robertson drove off for a business trip to Aberdeen, Scotland.

Buttons held on for dear life for six hours, until Robertson stopped at a service station in Newcastle. He lifted the hood to check on the oil. To his stunned surprise, Robertson found the cat, covered with grime, crouching behind the battery. "How she survived six hours of nonstop driving, I will never know," he said. "The engine was incredibly hot, and what with the fumes, smoke, and noise, it must have been a terrible experience for her."

Robertson fed the cat at a nearby restaurant and then continued his trip—this time with Buttons curled up in the backseat of his car. When he reached Aberdeen, Robertson phoned the cat's owner with the news about Buttons.

Ever since, Buttons has stayed far away from cars.

CHIPS, CANDY, OR A CAT?

Curiosity almost killed Shadow the cat.

In 1990, Shadow disappeared shortly after her owner, Daresa Hooper of Grafton, Virginia, sold six empty snack machines to J. R. Hilton, owner of a vending business in nearby Chesapeake. Somehow, Shadow had managed to sneak into one of the machines when Hilton removed the back to inspect the parts inside.

The 5-foot-tall (1.5-meter) candy vending machine was taken to Chesapeake, where it was stored outside under a tarp for more than a month, waiting to be resold. Meanwhile, Hooper searched all over town for her missing cat.

More than a month later, Hooper realized that the last time she had seen Shadow, the cat was sniffing around the vending machines that had been sold to Hilton. Could Shadow have ended up trapped in one of them? It seemed ridiculous, but she had run out of ideas. So she called Hilton and asked him to inspect the machines.

He did. Sure enough, there was Shadow! "I opened the door to one of the machines and saw these two very blue eyes staring at me," recalled Hilton. "Then it let out three big yowls."

Amazingly, the cat had survived without food or water for thirty-seven days! Although she lost about 3 pounds (1.4 kilograms) and was dehydrated from her ordeal, Shadow was bright and alert. She was soon returned home, where she stayed very close to her mistress.

TROUBLE SHOOTER

A dog shot her master with a rifle—but she didn't mean to do it.

The bizarre incident happened in 1991 in St. Laurent, Manitoba, Canada, shortly after Joe Petrowski, thirty-two, had cleaned and adjusted the sight of a long-barreled .22-caliber rifle. Handling his weapon in the backyard, Petrowski had removed the metal guard underneath the trigger and fastened the rifle to a portable workbench.

The back end of the rifle, including the exposed trigger, extended out from the workbench.

Petrowski began shooting at a target 30 yards (27.5 meters) away. His one-year-old German shepherd, Vegas, was by his side. After his final shot, Petrowski reloaded the rifle and went to check the target.

Meanwhile, Vegas walked under the back end of the rifle. The top of her back brushed against the exposed trigger. The gun went off with her master, who was facing the target, directly in the line of fire.

Petrowski was shot in the back. Because no one else was home at the time, Petrowski crawled back to the house and phoned for help. Despite being shot, he still kept his sense of humor. "The gal on the phone didn't believe me when I told her the shooting involved a dog," he recalled. "So I told her, 'Don't worry, the dog doesn't know how to reload.'"

Petrowski was rushed to the hospital and made a full recovery. As for Vegas, her master said, "I still love her. She didn't mean to shoot me."

BOOK HOUND

A golden retriever named Wofford loved to sink his teeth into a good book. Unfortunately, his fondness for the written word landed him in court.

Wofford, owned by David Viccellio of Norfolk, Virginia, had a thing about books. "Our family likes to read, so there are books everywhere," explained Viccellio. "Whenever a guest comes over, Wofford will pick up a book with his teeth and hand it to him. He just loves books, especially paperbacks." Other times, the book hound would curl up in a corner with a good book.

One day in 1993, the dog slipped through a broken slat in the backyard fence and wandered into the library next door. Seeing all those books, Wofford couldn't resist. He snatched a children's book off a little table and, being a friendly pooch, headed over to where all the people were gathered, at the checkout counter.

One of the librarians called the phone number on Wofford's collar, but no one was home. So she left a message: "This is the library. Your dog is trying to check out a book and he doesn't have a card."

Viccellio showed up at the library moments before Wofford was about to be hauled off to the pound. The owner was given his pet—and a summons to appear in court for having a loose dog and not having a dog license. The judge dropped the charges against the dog but ordered Viccellio to pay court costs of $28.

Reading about the zany case in the newspapers, students at an elementary school in Virginia Beach, Virginia, gave Wofford a gift—his very own school library card.

MAKE NO BONES ABOUT IT, HE'S A SHOPLIFTER

Rocky the St. Bernard was arrested and thrown in the slammer for five days on a charge of shoplifting.

On a cold day in 1991, the 175-pound (79.5-kilogram) dog was pacing in front of the entrance to the RXD Pharmacy in Gloucester Township, New Jersey. One of the clerks felt sorry for the dog and let him inside.

Moments later, Rocky stopped at the pet food section. Then he saw something that had him drooling—a 99-cent,

2-pound (.9-kilogram) bag of Pet Pleasers rawhide bones. The pooch picked up a bag, then walked out an automatic door while customers watched in amazement.

The store manager called police, who cornered Rocky a short distance away from the store. But the dog thought they wanted to play, so he kept dodging them. He finally gave up when the dog catcher arrived.

"The suspect was definitely resisting arrest," said Sgt. Kenneth Saunders. "He didn't actually confess, but he still had the stolen goods with him. We can't read a dog his rights, so we handed him over to the Animal Orphanage."

Officials dropped the charges once they learned that Rocky had wandered away from home and become lost. They were convinced he had swiped the bones solely because he was hungry, not because he was a four-legged criminal.

JUST CALL 911-DOG

A playful puppy got collared by the cops after he called them on the phone.

The five-month-old mutt, named Ben, was home alone in Higham, England, in 1993 when he knocked the phone to the floor and began chewing on it. As he gnawed away, Ben randomly tapped out a police emergency number with his paws.

The operator who answered heard heavy breathing and a dog barking on the other end of the line. Thinking a victim was hurt and unable to speak, the operator notified police.

After the call was traced to the house, eight cops

arrived. Because the house was locked, police used a sledgehammer to smash in the front door. They rushed inside—and found Ben sitting in the corner, wagging his tail. The phone lay next to him. The cops gave Ben a pat on the head and then announced the case was closed.

DIAMOND IN THE RUFF

For a few hours, Duque (pronounced Duke) the mutt was worth $15,000. That was the value of the diamond ring he swallowed in one gulp.

In 1991, Carolyn Solomon took her ring to Creative Jewelers in Laguna Beach, California, to have it cleaned. Greeting her at the door was Duque, a friendly 60-pound (27-kilogram) black mixed-breed owned by jeweler Art Peltz.

Whenever Peltz cleaned jewelry, Duque would always playfully jump up and nip at the steam that sprayed out of the ring-cleaning machine. But on this day, Duque got carried away. When Peltz held Solomon's ring and waved it through the steam, Duque jumped up to take a bite of the spray—and gulped down the ring.

"I couldn't believe my eyes when the ring disappeared," Peltz recalled.

Once Solomon recovered from the shock of learning her valuable piece of jewelry was in the dog's stomach, she took Duque to an animal hospital and asked the vet for help. After taking an X-ray that showed the ring was in Duque's stomach, Dr. James Levin gave him a drink that made the dog throw up. Out flew the ring.

Peltz cleaned the ring again—but this time he made sure that Duque stayed in the front of the shop.

THE BARK WAS WORSE THAN THE BITE

Davey, a pit bull terrier, attacked and chewed thirteen trees on city property, causing $1,200 in damages.

It wasn't all his fault. He was only following orders.

In 1988, police discovered that several young trees in downtown Lancaster, Pennsylvania, had been severely damaged by teeth marks. An investigation eventually led authorities to Davey. Although he was considered harmless, his owner's nineteen-year-old nephew was arrested.

At the trial, the teen admitted he had told the dog to attack the trees as a way of showing him off to his friends. "It was much like having a dog fetch a stick," said the teen's lawyer, "except that the stick didn't move."

Davey got off, but the teen was sentenced to two years probation and forty hours of pruning and planting city trees.

THE BITE WAS WORSE THAN THE BARK

In 1992, the Van Hilst family of Belgium went to the pet store to buy a dog. The kids fell in love with a small gray puppy that looked very different from the other dogs.

They brought the pup home and named him Loupy. They liked playing with him, but no matter how hard they tried, they couldn't seem to housebreak or train him. Meanwhile, their pet kept growing bigger and bigger. Even worse, he was playing much rougher with the kids as he grew up, and the family couldn't make Loupy stay in their yard. He kept running off and returning with small animals he had caught.

In 1996, when the Van Hilsts took their pet to the veterinarian for a checkup, the vet gave them some startling news: Loupy was not a dog. He was a wolf!

NEVER STICK YOUR TONGUE OUT AT A TURTLE

In Mississippi in 1996, a five-year-old boy got down on his hands and knees, got nose-to-nose with a turtle—and stuck his tongue out.

Apparently, the turtle didn't think that was very nice. It snapped onto the boy's tongue and wouldn't let go!

When Alcorn County Emergency 911 received a call that a turtle had a boy by the tongue, officials thought it was a prank. But when the ambulance arrived, paramedics saw otherwise. They got a pail of water and had the boy lean over until his face was just above the surface. Then they held the turtle's head under the water. A few minutes later, the turtle let go.

The boy had only a slight cut on his tongue that didn't require any treatment. He promised never to stick his tongue out at another living thing again.

SURPRISE ATTACK

In 1992, David Rocque and his brother, Marc, of Melbourne, Florida, were fishing off the tip of Cape Canaveral. Suddenly, a 6-foot (1.8-meter) tarpon leaped out of the water.

But before the brothers could catch the big fish, it caught them. The tarpon leaped right into their 22-foot (6.7-meter) boat!

"I heard it come out of the water, and all I had time to do was scream," said David. "It hit me square in the chest, hard enough to knock me clear out of the boat."

Then the tarpon began thrashing inside the boat, breaking six fishing poles and a rodholder while Marc cringed up front. When the fish finally got tired, David climbed back into the boat. Then he and his brother picked up the fish and let it go free.

THE AVENGING FISH

In 1984, Mark Parker of Linton, Louisiana, caught a 2-pound (.9-kilogram) largemouth bass. He took it home, put it on a table, and began to clean it. Even though the fish was dead, it managed to get its revenge.

As Parker stuck his finger in the bass's mouth, the fisherman was bitten by a snake! Parker painfully discovered that just before he had caught the bass, it had swallowed a foot-long (30-centimeter) poisonous water moccasin, which had remained alive inside the bass. When Parker started to clean the bass, the snake slithered out of the fish's mouth and attacked him.

Parker killed the snake, then had to spend the night in the hospital for treatment of the bite.

SICK AND TIRED

LET'S SLEEP ON IT

A thirty-nine-year-old patient of Dr. Alan Searle of Port Orchard, Washington, was alarmed about suddenly developing an unexpected problem of bed-wetting.

But an examination revealed that the patient appeared to be in excellent health. Months later, when the patient returned with a different complaint, Dr. Searle asked if he had any further bed-wetting problems.

"Nope," said the patient, "not since we fixed the hole in the water bed."

IT'S A GROWTH PROBLEM

Dr. Chili Robinson of Corpus Christi, Texas, walked into the examining room, where a concerned mother told him that her son had a black growth on his neck. She was sure it had not been there weeks earlier.

As he examined the healthy boy, Dr. Robinson easily spotted the raised black growth on his neck. He had never seen anything like it in his medical textbooks.

Gingerly, the doctor touched the growth—then picked off the boy's dried chewing gum.

ONLY A MATTER OF TIME

One day, Dr. Jerome Schneyer of Southfield, Michigan, was escorting a visiting medical professor on morning rounds at the hospital. They had just left the room of a patient who truly believed he was about to die, even though he wasn't.

As the physicians were walking down the hall, the patient rushed after them. Going up to the professor, the patient pleaded, "Tell me the truth, Doc. How much time do I have left?"

The professor was still talking to Dr. Schneyer and didn't hear the question. The professor chose that exact moment to look down at his watch. The next thing the doctors knew, the patient had fainted on the hallway floor.

MISSING THE MARK

Nursing instructor Linda Rooda was watching a student try to give her first injection to a patient.

Hoping to calm the nervous student, instructor Rooda pinched the skin of the patient so the student would know exactly where to give the shot. She then watched in horror as the student swiftly plunged the needle off target. The needle went through the outstretched webbing of skin between Rooda's thumb and forefinger and into the patient. The student then depressed the plunger and removed the needle.

When the student discovered what she had done, she was so shocked and embarrassed that she hid in the bathroom for the rest of the afternoon.

PERHAPS YOU'RE A LITTLE TOO FOCUSED

Soon after nursing student Lisa Pitler learned the proper way to give a bath to a bedridden patient, she was assigned to her first nursing-home patient.

Seeing the elderly man was asleep, Pitler began to bathe him very carefully. She was washing his feet when her instructor entered the room and asked, "How's the bath going?"

"It's going just fine," Pitler replied.

"Has the patient moved or made any noise?"

"No," said Pitler. "He's been quiet and seems to be enjoying the bath."

The instructor took Pitler out into the hall and told her, "The patient you were bathing died several hours ago."

BLIND MAN'S BLUFF

A male patient of Dr. June T. Martin of Pittsfield, Massachusetts, needed special tests.

An X-ray technician led him into a room where a hospital gown was laid out near the head of the bed. "I'll wait for you at the end of the hall," she said. Pointing to the gown, she instructed, "Take off your clothes and put that on over your head."

Several minutes went by, and the technician became concerned when the patient failed to appear. She went back into the room and couldn't believe her eyes. There was the patient, wandering around the room, wearing only a pillowcase over his head!

DEAD TO THE WORLD

Serena Miller worked the midnight shift as an emergency-room clerk in the Vanderbilt University Medical Center in Nashville, Tennessee.

One night around 3:00 A.M., several obnoxious students walked in to watch the doctors and nurses in action. After trying unsuccessfully to get the students to leave, Miller dialed what she thought was the campus police.

When a sleepy male voice answered, Miller asked, "Would you come and pick up several people who are just lying around, cluttering up the emergency room?"

"How many are there?" he asked.

"We haven't bothered to count them."

After a long pause, the man said, "Lady, I sure hope you've got the wrong number. This is the Woodlawn Funeral Home."

SCREAMING FOR ATTENTION

When Jayne Smith went into labor in 1993 in San Jose, California, she let out a terrifying scream. It sent her husband, Jake, scrambling for the car keys so he could rush her to the hospital.

He put her in the backseat and told her to lie down. But Jayne felt like sitting up. As the car squealed out of the driveway, Jayne rolled down the window and stuck her head out, trying to stay cool.

As each contraction hit, she let loose with one of her ear-shattering screams and pounded the side of the car with her fist. Meanwhile, Jake, going as fast as possible, came to a red light. Seeing no cross traffic, he sped on through.

Imagine what the woman standing on the corner just

witnessed: a speeding car running a red light and a woman screaming in the backseat. The woman dashed into the nearest store and phoned 911. She told the dispatcher what she had seen and described the car.

As Jake wheeled his car—with his screaming wife leaning out the back window—to the front of the emergency room, a police car pulled in right behind him. With one hand on his revolver, the cop was about to yell, "Halt!" Then he heard Jake shout to an orderly, "My wife is having a baby!" The officer kept his hand on the weapon until he saw Jayne, in pain, helped to a waiting wheelchair.

Noticing the cop for the first time, Jake said, "I could have used you back there."

"You're lucky none of us saw you earlier, or you might have had your tires shot out," replied the officer. "You were a suspect in a possible kidnapping!"

AN ARRESTING DEVELOPMENT

When Angie Cottrell went into labor in 1995, her husband, Steve, tried not to panic. As gently as he could, he put his wife into the car and sped off toward the hospital in Madison, Wisconsin, 10 miles (16 kilometers) away.

As the car roared through the town of Monona, the couple saw flashing lights in the rearview mirror. "Oh, great, honey," Angie told Steve. "The police are pulling us over. Once we explain why we're speeding, they'll probably give us an escort to the hospital."

Officer Frank Fenton stopped their car, came to the driver's window, and informed Steve that he was going 80 miles (129 kilometers) an hour in a 55-mile-an-hour (88-kilometer) zone.

"But, Officer," said Steve, pointing to Angie, "my wife is having a baby, and I've got to get her to the hospital!"

"You're not going anywhere, pal," the officer said. "You're getting a ticket for speeding."

Frantic that Angie would give birth at any moment, Steve made a big mistake. He drove away. Officer Fenton then radioed for help, saying he was chasing a suspect. The cop didn't tell fellow officers about Angie's pregnancy.

As the Cottrells got closer to the hospital, more and more policemen followed the couple's speeding car. Then, at a red light, a police car pulled in front of them and blocked their path.

With their guns drawn, several cops ran up to the open window on the driver's side. They grabbed Steve by the shirt, pulled him out of the car, and handcuffed him. That's when they noticed Angie's condition—and rushed her to the hospital.

After Steve was given his ticket, he was released and allowed to join his wife in the delivery room. Angie soon gave birth to a healthy 6-pound, 9-ounce (3-kilogram) boy.

When Monona mayor Tom Metcalfe learned of the ordeal that the police had put the Cottrells through, he apologized. He also sent them a bouquet of flowers and tore up the traffic ticket.

YOO HOO, REMEMBER ME?

While she was visiting Philadelphia, Vicky Porter of Washington, D.C., went into labor six weeks early.

Porter called her personal doctor in Washington. He told her to get to the nearest hospital in Philadelphia. Then he leaped into his car and drove 130 miles (209 kilometers) to Vicky's hospital.

By the time her doctor arrived, Porter already had been taken into the delivery room. Although her doctor didn't have privileges at the hospital, he managed to talk his way into the delivery room.

Porter was happy to see him. The attending doctor was not. One word led to another concerning who was in charge of this birth, and soon the two doctors were shoving each other.

While Vicky watched the battle with astonishment, she started giving birth. Between her pains, she blurted out, "Hey, guys, the baby is here! Could one of you please stop shoving a minute and catch it?"

DRIVEN TO DISTRACTION

A bus driver became so grossed out as he listened to a passenger describe an operation that he passed out at the wheel. The bus then plowed into eight parked cars.

Details of the bizarre 1993 accident were revealed in court in Liverpool, England.

Bus driver Michael Lount told the judge that he can't stand the sight of blood. He said he became queasy when a passenger launched into a graphic account of her recent surgery. Her story caused him to faint before he could step on the brakes.

Nevertheless, the judge put the blame for the crash on the driver. The judge ruled that Lount should not have listened to the unpleasant story while driving the bus. The bus company was ordered to pay damages to the owners of the cars that the bus struck.

BEARERS OF BAD TIDINGS

A determined ambulance crew arrived at a house, forced a man onto a stretcher, strapped him down despite his objections, and rushed him to the hospital.

Only then did the crew realize their man had a real beef. This guy was healthy—and angry. The crew had gone to the wrong house and picked up the wrong guy!

It happened in 1995 near Oslo, Norway. "I tried to protest when the ambulance came," the man recalled. "But I was told that from then on they were making the decisions and I had no say in it."

It turned out that the healthy man and the sick man both had the same name, lived in the same village, and had been to the same hospital for tests. That's why the ambulance crew got confused.

When the ambulance failed to show for the sick man, he managed to drive himself to the hospital. But when he arrived, the hospital at first refused to admit him. The clerk insisted the poor fellow was already there!

BAD FOR BUSINESS

LANGUAGE PROBLEM

When companies try to sell their products in a foreign country, sometimes their advertising message gets lost in the translation. For example:

• PepsiCo ran an ad campaign in Germany featuring the slogan, "the come-alive generation." But in the German translation, the slogan came out as "the arise-from-the-grave generation." Consumers in Germany wondered if Pepsi was some kind of drink for zombies.

• Coca-Cola Co. had to change its name in China in 1986 after it discovered that, when spoken in Chinese, its name meant "Bite the wax tadpole."

• General Motors Corp. couldn't understand why sales of its new economy car, the Nova, were so bad in Latin America. Finally, GM wised up and realized that in Spanish, "No va" means "It doesn't go."

AN A-PEELING SALES PITCH

In 1986, Silo, a discount appliance-store chain, ran a TV commercial for a stereo it claimed cost only "299 bananas." Obviously, the store used the word *bananas* as slang for dollars.

Nevertheless, dozens of customers in Seattle, Washington, and El Paso, Texas, took the commercial at its word. Each of thirty-six customers brought 299 bananas into a Silo store and demanded a stereo.

Silo had no choice but to honor the fruity money. The chain lost over $10,000 on the stereos. But they gained nearly 11,000 bananas.

By the way, Silo gave up using slang in its commercials.

AT LEAST IT GOT PEOPLE INTO THE LIBRARY

For a 1994 promotion, Dallas, Texas, radio station KYNG announced that it had hidden five- and ten-dollar bills in the pages of novels in the fiction section of the Fort Worth Central Library.

Within a matter of minutes, the peaceful library was invaded by hordes of money-hungry people. They ran into the library, screaming, "Where's fiction? Where's fiction?"

More than five hundred KYNG listeners streamed into the aisles of the fiction section. They ransacked the shelves, thumbing through pages, dumping books, bumping into each other, and squealing when they found money.

When it was all over, more than 3,500 books were on the floor, many with their spines cracked, pages torn, and covers ripped. At least 100 books were beyond repair.

KYNG promised to come up with a different promotion next time.

A BAD HAIR DAY

Toy manufacturer Mattel, Inc., thought it had come up with a wonderful new product—the Cabbage Patch Snacktime Doll. The doll had a motorized mouth that ate plastic food.

Before manufacturing the dolls, Mattel made a few models that were tested at a California child-care center. Once the company engineers were satisfied that the doll was absolutely safe, Mattel made 500,000 dolls for the holiday season in 1996.

Parents snatched the dolls off the shelves. It looked like Mattel, the makers of the Barbie doll, had another hit. But then the company received a mouthful of bad news.

Some of the dolls were eating more than the plastic french fries, celery, and other tidbits they were supposed to gobble down.

The dolls were eating little girls' hair!

Every day, Mattel received new reports of a girl whose hair accidentally got caught in the doll's chomping mouth. Unable to stop the doll's chewing, frantic parents had no choice but to cut their child's hair to free her from the hungry doll. "It was a nightmare," said one South Carolina parent. "The doll ripped a patch of hair right out of my daughter's scalp."

Parents couldn't turn off the doll because Mattel had decided against an on-off safety switch. The company also failed to tell consumers that they could shut off the doll by removing its backpack.

Within days, Mattel was forced to pull the $40 dolls from the store shelves and offer a full refund to customers. The hot seller suddenly became history.

Rather than change the doll's design so that it would no longer have an appetite for hair, Mattel chose not to sell it anymore. The company ate millions of dollars in lost sales.

Moaned Mattel executive Jim Walter, "I just wish we'd seen this problem coming before we put the doll in the stores."

SUCKING UP A BIG LOSS

The Maytag Corporation ran a promotion in England and Ireland that nearly cleaned out its bank account.

In 1993, advertisements offered customers two free airline tickets with each Hoover vacuum cleaner bought. Sales skyrocketed, requiring the company to put its workers on overtime to produce enough vacuums. Still, Maytag was barely able to meet the demand.

That seemed like a nice position for a company to be in. So what was the problem?

Whoever came up with the promotion must have flunked math. The airline tickets were worth up to $600, but the vacuums sold for as little as $165. Which meant that for every vacuum sold, the company was losing as much as $435!

Maytag announced the goof would cost the company $30 million. It was wrong. By the end of 1996, it had paid out a whopping $72 million in airline tickets.

STUCK UP

As a promotion in 1993, Taco Bell gave away little puppets that were supposed to stick to your finger.

But the promotional toys, including Lowly Worm and Huckle Cat finger puppets, were recalled. Why? Too many kids stuck the puppets on their tongues and couldn't get them off without lots of discomfort.

Customers who returned the puppets were given something that was extremely tongue-friendly—free tacos.

THE SOFT DRINK THAT EXPLODED ON THE MARKET

Napa Natural was called "the world's first natural soft drink"—a can't-miss product that *did* miss because of one little problem.

The drink, a combination of bottled water and fruit juice, became an instant hit in 1984 when it was introduced to the public. Sales soared. The Adams Natural Beverage Co. was enjoying the sweet taste of success. Then life soured.

Stores began reporting that the cans of Napa Natural were bulging and often blowing their lids right on the shelves! The company realized it had forgotten to consider that the drink would ferment (sour and bubble) because of the high juice content and lack of preservatives. The fermentation eventually caused the cans to explode.

The company was forced to recall thousands of cases of Napa Natural. It changed the content of the drink, but many supermarket chains refused to take the product back. Sales of the drink soon fizzled.

IDEAS DOOMED FROM THE START

Many new products flopped because companies didn't do their homework. Had they asked us, we would have told them their product wouldn't sell. For example:

In 1981, Gerber Products Co., makers of baby food, came up with a line of products aimed at the teen market.

It was called Gerber Desserts. Puddings and fruit were put in large baby jars. The company ran ads in teen magazines saying, "The secret's out. Gerber isn't just for babies!"

But teens refused to bite.

* * *

In the early 1970s, Frank Aldridge, president of American Kitchen Foods, thought he had come up with a terrific idea: Mash vegetables into the shape of french fries so picky kids would eat their veggies.

Soon American Kitchen was shipping frozen packages of "I Hate Peas," "I Hate Beets," and "I Hate Spinach" disguised as french fries. Mothers snatched them off the grocery shelves.

But the nation's kids realized instantly that peas still tasted like peas, no matter what shape they were in. They refused to touch the new product with a ten-foot fork.

* * *

Here are some other products that bombed:
- Gorilla Balls protein supplement snack
- Buffalo Chip chocolate cookies
- To-Fitness Tofu Pasta
- Parsnip Chips
- Norwoods Egg Coffee
- A Touch of Yogurt Shampoo
- Gimme Cucumber hair conditioner
- Chocolate Styling Gel

EVERY DOG HAS HIS DAY

In the mid 1960s, the public relations firm Harshe & Rotman, Inc., barked up the wrong tree when it tried to promote Rival dog food's new all-beef dinner.

The agency decided to invite the press to a luncheon where the president of Rival and a pedigreed dog would share a table. "I felt uneasy about it because I know that animals can be very unpredictable," recalled Morris Rotman, head of the public relations firm. "I was assured that the dog, a collie, was well-trained and would be hungry."

With reporters on hand to witness the man-and-his-dog luncheon, the collie did what Rotman feared most—it turned up its nose at the new Rival food. No amount of coaxing could get the dog to even sniff the bowl.

Finally, in desperation, the Rival president reached into the bowl and ate the stuff himself—to the cheers of the reporters.

The next day, the newspapers carried stories with headlines such as "Rival President Eats Dog Food, But Dog Won't." Rotman's humiliated client took one look at the publicity and fired the agency. Said Rotman, "I've never used an animal since."

THEY SAID IT WOULD NEVER FLY

A commuter airline called Pacific Air Lines wanted an attention-grabbing advertising campaign that would get business soaring. Instead, PAL ran a promotion that sent the company into a tailspin.

In 1967, comedian and ad consultant Stan Freberg suggested PAL poke fun at the one thing airlines never mention—fear of flying.

Under the comedian's direction, PAL placed full-page ads that read, "Hey, there! You with the sweat in your palms. It's about time an airline faced up to something: most people are scared witless of flying. Deep down inside, every time that big plane lifts off that runway, you wonder if this is it, right? You want to know something, fella? So does the pilot deep down inside."

At Freberg's urging, PAL didn't stop there. It added some zany touches on its flights to help people laugh at their fears. Flight attendants gave passengers survival kits that contained a pink rabbit's foot and the book *The Power of Positive Thinking*. Also, whenever the plane touched down, flight attendants were told to say in loud voices, "We made it! How about that?"

To give shaky airborne passengers a feeling that they were still on the ground, PAL planned to draw the cabin shades and project pictures of telephone poles going by. PAL also planned to paint one of its jets to look like an old steam locomotive and broadcast the sounds of a train throughout the passenger cabin.

Not surprisingly, the promotion did the exact opposite of what it intended. It scared potential customers away from the airline. Within two months, PAL went out of business.

OPPORTUNITY KNOCKED, BUT NO ONE ANSWERED

When the Beatles auditioned for Decca Records in 1962, the record executives refused to sign the new group because they didn't like its sound.

Decca bigwig Dick Rose told Beatles manager Brian Epstein, "Groups with guitars are on their way out." The foursome's manager begged Decca to reconsider and promised he would personally buy three thousand copies of any single his group recorded. But Decca turned a deaf ear to the Beatles.

The group signed with EMI Records . . . and the rest is history.

✸　✸　✸

When Alexander Graham Bell invented the telephone in 1876, it did not ring the bells of potential investors. His company, Bell Telephone Co., was so desperate for cash that it offered to sell all the patents to the telephone to Western Union for $100,000.

But Western Union said it had no use for "an electrical toy." Hello?

✸　✸　✸

In 1975, a low-level Hewlett-Packard engineer named Steve Wozniak shared a dream with his pal Steven Jobs—to build and sell a personal computer for home and school use.

The pair tinkered together to create a compact PC. Their invention was offered to Hewlett-Packard, which turned down the idea. So Wozniak and Jobs went off on their own, founded Apple Computer, Inc., and helped revolutionize the personal computer industry.

MELTS IN YOUR MOUTH, NOT IN E.T.'S HANDS

While filming the classic movie *E.T.*, the producers asked the M&M/Mars Company for permission to use M&Ms in the film. The company said no.

Elliot wound up luring the lovable alien with Hershey's Reese's Pieces. That scene also wound up luring millions of kids into the stores to buy Reese's Pieces. Thanks to the megahit, Hershey's sales shot up 65 percent.

THE NAME GAME

There was a popular restaurant in Chicago in the 1970s called The Great Gritzbe's Flying Food Show. But by 1983, business wasn't so great. So owner Richard Melman changed the name of the restaurant to The Not So Great Gritzbe's.

Apparently, customers took his word for it. They stopped coming to the restaurant. Three months after the name change, the business closed its doors.

ANY WONDER WHY THESE LOSERS DIDN'T GET JOBS?

When you get older and go on a job interview, there's one thing you definitely should not do—act like a loser. A 1996 survey of personnel directors of the nation's top corporations revealed that some people have no clue how to behave when they're trying to get a job.

Among the worst job candidates were those who did one of the following:

• Challenged the interviewer to arm wrestle.

• Claimed he had never finished high school because he had been kidnapped and kept in a closet in Mexico.

• Wore headphones to the interview and, when asked to remove them, said she could listen to the interviewer and the music at the same time.

• Said she didn't have time for lunch and started to eat a hamburger and fries in the interviewer's office.

• Fell and broke his arm during the interview.

- Interrupted the interview to phone her therapist for advice in answering a question.

- Dozed off during the interview.

- Refused to sit down and insisted on being interviewed standing up.

- Asked, "Would it be a problem if I'm angry most of the time?"

✳ ✳ ✳

Then there is the hard-luck story of Salim Roy of Calcutta.

For two years, the forty-two-year-old man had been trying to find work without success. However, he didn't give up. At the hiring office of a plastics company in 1996, Roy finally heard the words he yearned for: "We'd like to hire you."

Roy was so excited at getting his first job since 1994 that he yelled in triumph—then keeled over and died.

OUT OF TIME

André-François Raffray, a lawyer from Arles, France, thought he had made the deal of a lifetime.

In 1965, he signed a contract giving Jeanne Calment, who was then 90 years old, $500 a month for life—on the condition that he would get her house when she died. Believing Calment's days were numbered, the 47-year-old Raffray figured he would soon own a house for very little money.

Raffray waited and waited for Calment to die. Ten

years passed . . . 20 years . . . 30 . . . and Calment was still going strong! In February 1996, she celebrated her 121st birthday, making her the oldest known living person in the world.

Ten months later, Raffray died at the age of 77. Before his death, he said, "We all make bad deals in life. This was mine." He had paid Calment more than $180,000 for a house worth no more than $60,000—a house he never got to own.